COMMON
SENSE

By Tony Benn

The Regeneration of Britain
Speeches
Arguments for Socialism
Arguments for Democracy
Parliament, People and Power
The Sizewell Syndrome
Fighting Back: Speaking Out for Socialism in the Eighties
Out of the Wilderness: Diaries 1963–1967
Office Without Power: Diaries 1968–1972
Against the Tide: Diaries 1973–1976
Conflicts of Interest: Diaries 1977–1980
The End of an Era: Diaries 1980–1990
A Future for Socialism

COMMON SENSE

A New Constitution for Britain

Tony Benn & Andrew Hood

Edited by Ruth Winstone

HUTCHINSON
London

This edition first published in 1993 by
Hutchinson

Random House (UK) Ltd
20 Vauxhall Bridge Road, London SW1V 2SA

Random House Australia (Pty) Ltd
20 Alfred Street, Milsons Point, Sydney, NSW 2061, Australia

Random House New Zealand Ltd
18 Poland Road, Glenfield, Auckland 10, New Zealand

Random House South Africa (Pty) Ltd
PO Box 337, Bergvlei, 2012, South Africa

A CIP record for this book is
available from the British Library

ISBN 0 09 177308 3

Set in Plantin by Falcon Graphic Art Ltd, Wallington Surrey
Printed and bound in Great Britain by Clays Ltd, St Ives PLC

Contents

Acknowledgements

Common Sense is the product of close collaboration with Andrew Hood going back over several years. We talked through the issues at great length in the preparation of this book and the associated constitutional reform bills which are its core.

His deep analysis of the relationships deriving from the power of capital and its effect on human rights has broadened the argument to cover areas often overlooked when the constitution is discussed.

It fell to Ruth Winstone to integrate our individual contributions – an almost impossible task – and the book could never have been completed without her.

I am most indebted to Anthony Whittome for his encouragement, support and critical comment and to Neil Bradford for enabling *Common Sense* to be published so quickly.

Tony Benn

I could hardly be more grateful for Ruth Winstone's help and patience, and to Alan Davies for many perceptive suggestions and inspiring conversations. Katheryn Macvarish, Damian White and Ian Jermyn collectively provided a sounding board for ideas and invaluable feedback.

Alison, Catherine and Simon Hood all deserve my thanks for their support, food parcels and financial aid. I am very grateful to Simon Tucker, who made a serious job more entertaining, to Danny Freidman and Mick Gordon, and to my patient students at Wentworth Tutors.

Ben Laurence and Martin Jacques provided early suggestions and ideas for research and I am also grateful to Ben Pimlott; and to Lord Wilson for permission to use his correspondence.

Finally, thanks to Tony for inspiration and partnership in a difficult but worthwhile project.

Andrew Hood

Foreword

The 'Mother of Parliaments' is, we have been told for far too long, the envy of the world.

Such self-delusion has almost blinded us to the fact that over the past forty years Britain has been increasingly seen as a comic and antiquated Ruritania attracting the curiosity of tourists but lacking self-respect or self-criticism.

But the long-term decline of Britain, its manufacturing industry and its economy, and the weakening of its social cohesion, have inevitably led to fundamental questions about the relationship between our present parlous state and the nature of the British constitution.

What is its nature? Britain, the text books say, is a constitutional monarchy. In practice it is a feudal state upholding and entwined with a series of public institutions. There is now a rapidly growing cynicism about these 'great' institutions – the Crown, Parliament and the civil service, the mass media and the financial establishment. The public confidence on which their authority has hitherto rested has been thoroughly shaken.

This cynicism is dangerous because it breeds arrogance on the part of those who govern without popular consent and defeatism and demoralisation in those whom the government and its agencies ignore.

Such an atmosphere of defeatism could easily prepare the way for a very unpleasant authoritarianism in which demagogues seek to fill the moral vacuum with appeals to sweep away the apparatus of this 'decadent democracy'.

The time has come to refound our public institutions upon the principles of the common weal, democracy and an internationalism more in tune with the needs of the 21st century.

It is the core of this argument that Britain should become a republic, replacing the feudal structures inherited from the past with democratic institutions for the future.

The Commonwealth of Britain Bill, discussed in this book, addresses these problems.

The most important change in law and practice would be that every Briton would become a citizen of a democratic, federal and secular commonwealth dedicated to the welfare of all and with fundamental human rights enshrined in a charter dealing with political, legal, social and economic dimensions.

The Bill makes the case for a far greater devolution of power from London to Scotland, Wales and the English regions and for the reestablishment of local government answerable to the people it serves.

It provides for votes at sixteen and for the equal representation of the sexes in Parliament by ensuring that every constituency would elect one man and one woman to the Commons.

It would end the role of the Crown, replacing the monarch with an elected President as head of state and all oaths of allegiance to the Crown would disappear in favour of one common oath to uphold the constitution.

The Bill would replace the House of Lords with a House of the People and substitute an accountable Council of State for the Privy Council.

It would provide for a far-reaching reform of our legal system under which the magistrates would be elected, the High Court judges would have to be confirmed after nomination and police forces would be responsible to their local authorities.

It would include the framework for a Freedom of Information Act and the parliamentary supervision of the security services.

The separation of church and state would be entrenched in the Bill to allow the established Church of England full freedom to decide its structure and faith and choose its own leaders, and thereby ensure the equality before the law of those of all faiths and to end for ever the common law of blasphemy.

The associated Commonwealth of Europe Bill would bring the foreign relations of Britain, including our relations with the European Community, the United Nations and other treaty allies including those in NATO, under Parliamentary control.

This book identifies the source of the present discontent as a stagnant feudalism which seeks to subdue the country and make it an instrument of the demands of international capital.

In short it is an appeal for a great public debate about the future, and an invitation to the citizens of Britain to share the responsibility for the welfare of our country and its relations with the rest of the world.

Tony Benn
April 1993

I

The Decay of Britain

A long habit of not thinking a thing wrong gives it a superficial appearance of being right, and raises at first a formidable outcry in defence of custom. But the tumult soon subsides. Time makes more converts than reason.

Tom Paine, 1776

Any proposal for constitutional reform must address the central question. Who would gain and who would lose by it?

The losers would be those in whose name power in Britain is centralised, secretive and unaccountable; the winners, those who would benefit from a thorough extension of democracy within public and private institutions.

There is now a wide measure of agreement that Britain's social and economic decline has been happening for most of this century. It is the contention of this book that this decline is the responsibility of those at the top, who have held power and presided for so long over the institutions under which Britain is governed. The extraordinary feature of this system is that these governors have half-persuaded the governed that it is they who are responsible.

The industrial deterioration of Britain this century has undoubtedly been affected by the costs, human and otherwise, of two world wars – wars which diminished and destroyed an empire; at the same time world market forces have gradually eroded our manufacturing base, so that by 1990 an economic slump perhaps more serious than that experienced in the Thirties brought back mass unemployment and a widening disparity between the richest and the poorest, undermining the social cohesion which was taken for granted by governments since 1945.

British government, operating within essentially feudal structures, was unable to respond to these factors. It did not invest to re-equip, arguing that it did not need to in good years, and could not afford to in bad years; so that de-industrialisation set in by a process of ratcheting down the productive potential of the nation, a process not fundamentally halted by the national planning attempts of the 1960s and 70s. Public ownership did save industries – the railways, mines and some engineering that would otherwise have been lost, achievements which we should never underestimate. But nationalisation of the kind practised by the post-war Labour governments was centralised and reflected the same feudal values of British capitalism. Boards were appointed by ministers, not elected, and their managerial style was imperious and secretive, modelled more upon public institutions like the army or the Church than on any more democratic structures. And when public investment had put the industries on their feet, they were put up for sale to a new set of private owners.

Thus historically industry and commerce as they have developed have drawn heavily upon the political structures which preceded capitalism, with power concentrated at the top in the modern day squires and landlords, and the labour done by the serfs and servants at the bottom.

2

THE DECAY OF BRITAIN

Latterly, this industrial and commercial framework has been disciplined by powerful international financial institutions which use the low-wage third world as an instrument to reduce wages in Britain, a practice endorsed by the Conservative governments since the 1980s. Given the emphasis by such governments on the need for Britain to become industrially competitive, it is astonishing how little news coverage there was or is of industrial production, compared to every minor fluctuation in currencies or share values from hour to hour; the British economy has come to resemble a hypochondriac having its temperature and pulse taken twenty times a day.

The culture of subservience inculcated by this peculiar feudal and hierarchical history, and the resulting social cohesion which successive governments have assumed existed (which may have been more imaginary than real) certainly led people to accept their situation in the belief that it could be changed peacefully, by parliamentary means.

Thus the democratic process in Britain has tended to focus on the House of Commons and on political parties and their leaders, and the electorate has become a spectator of the process, regaled by exchanges across the chamber and satisfied with the assurance that the power to change it would come on polling day.

That we live in a real democracy is indeed something of an illusion. A cursory comparison between the rights of an American and a Briton shows that in the United States everyone votes for the head of state, both Houses of Congress and the state legislatures; in Britain only the House of Commons is re-elected, the Lords being filled by patronage or inheritance of an earlier patronage, while the head of state is hereditary, unchallenged and unchallengeable.

The hierarchy which derives its legitimacy from this system induces this deference from which no-one is entirely free. It accustoms people to take orders from their social superiors who are, it is assumed, imbued with special qualities of leadership, character and intelligence. People have become used to placing trust in their leaders, experts, officials and pundits to take decisions for them. This culture is reflected faithfully by the media, and the general willingness to delegate political decisions to professionals who endorse the status quo is typified by the media's political coverage, particularly the BBC's.

The BBC, nationalised by the Conservatives for much the same reason that the Church of England was nationalised, is overcentralised, hierarchical, and serves to promote a single authoritative voice and ethos. What is now needed is disestablishment of the BBC. Without a substantial decentralisation of editorial control the BBC hierarchy will remain immensely powerful and conservative. News and current affairs is presented on the BBC from an 'objective standpoint', ie that if coverage is criticised from the right and left its governors can therefore claim that they have found a balanced approach. Objectivity is virtually meaningless, but a truly 'balanced' approach would not be the presentation of a consensus view, reflecting the interests of the finance-obsessed Eighties and Nineties, but one which reflects all shades of opinion. Interestingly in religious broadcasting the BBC respects all denominations and faiths, but in political coverage neither pacifism, nor republicanism, nor socialism are treated as views worthy of fair representation.

The promotion of orthodoxy by the media is nowhere more evident than in coverage of the economy. The coverage of days lost through industrial disputes is published, but not days lost each year for all reasons. Each day that passes with four million unemployed, means the loss of four

4

million days production. A billion days of production lost a year. The withdrawal of investment – the closing down of a factory – is never called a strike of capital. There is no parallel drawn between workers who, after a ballot, vote to close a factory for a day, and a multinational which without consultation and at a week's notice closes a factory for ever. The language of news coverage is the language of capitalist values. But there are alternative views of major issues, within a capitalist-led culture.

The cultural values of capitalism are engendered by a mass medium of powerful newspaper proprietors and anyone who challenges their conventional wisdom is quickly singled out.

A glance at a *Times* editorial during the 1984 miners' strike, a campaign to prevent pit closures, makes the point:

> 'There is a war on. It is an undeclared civil war instigated by Mr Scargill, his squads of pickets and his political associates against the rest of society. The challenge can be met in only one way if the value of democracy and liberty under the law are to prevail – by enforcing the surrender of Mr Scargill and the . . . mineworkers' union' etc.

Today all coverage of news and current affairs is refracted through the eyes of 'experts' who present their own interpretation and reflect particular interests, and whose message is *there is no alternative*.

Meanwhile, a monarchy presides over Britain, supposedly above political controversy, exempt from any pressures by special interest, while at the same time the ultimate guarantor of 'democratic rights'.

The established church, too, acts as a reassuring influence in that its archbishops and bishops seek to unite the nation, whatever economic and political factors they may recognise as dividing it, whilst the House of Lords is seen to be above party, full of wisdom, in which balanced and independent judgement serves to uphold the Queen's peace.

Those who have made assaults on the right of the House of Lords as an unelected body are quickly reminded that it is the pedestal on which the monarchy rests and that any attempt to undermine the authority of the Lords would bring the Crown tumbling to the gutter, leading to anarchy and chaos in which the mob would rule. For 200 years, any attempts to bring democratic changes to either House have been met with the bugbear of mob rule.

Against this hierarchical system and the accompanying undemocratic institutional power of the Lords and Crown that has existed for centuries is set one day in every five years on which everyone enjoys absolutely equal political power; power which in theory could be used to change the policies, the personalities and even the structures and economic framework within which individuals live.

Despite all its limitations, that electoral right to remove unpopular governments without bloodshed and therefore to force them to listen to popular opinion between elections, represents an enormous gain on more dictatorial monarchies or regimes which existed or exist in the world. But since the 1960s and the time when Labour and Conservative teams would take turns in governing, there has been a realisation that fundamental constitutional reform is required in this cosy consensus, not Royal Commissions composed of the same big-wigs who have already been in power, newspaper articles, and television and radio documentaries.

There are those who believe that proportional representation is the answer to reform. But proportional representation would in practise merely consolidate the unofficial coalition which now exists into a formal one, and place greater power in the hands of those party leaders responsible for drawing up lists of candidates. Others argue that the nation state is finished and Britain will only prosper in a federal Europe, with an independent bank to enforce disciplines on us and with Commissioners free from electoral pressures to run capitalism from Brussels, much as the Soviet Communist Party ran communism from Moscow.

The proposals in the Commonwealth of Britain Bill are based on the conviction that the decay stems from lack of democracy in political and economic life; and *that* must be examined before any but a marginal change can be made in Britain's future prospects. Once the undemocratic nature of the golden triangle of the City, Whitehall and Parliament is laid bare, power can be wrested from it and diffused downwards and outwards.

The Growth of Cynicism

One of the effects of the seeming inability to resolve practical social and economic problems has been a widespread growth of cynicism. This cynicism extends to the role of Parliament itself.

The House of Commons is now widely considered to have abandoned its prime responsibility as a legislature and to have degenerated into a body of party machines, Her Majesty's Government and Her Majesty's Loyal Opposition instructing their members as to how to behave and vote, using the carrots of promotion and honours, or expulsion in turn.

The maintenance of a government in power has always been regarded as the prime duty of the governing party and this has led to increasing centralisation of the political party machines. Even though in opposition, the current Parliamentary Labour Party is not very different. The party leadership is now in a position to impose its will through the National Executive and the party's annual conference, and in constituencies. Here, active members have become merely contributors of cash and are voting fodder in the selection and election of compliant candidates who can be relied upon to support that leadership on entering the House of Commons.

Altogether, there is a logjam in British society driving people to apathy, despair and occasional outbreaks of illegality or even violence. But the Peasants' Revolt of 1381, the English Revolution of 1649, the cooperative movement, the great 19th-century pioneers of municipal government, universal suffrage and the successful campaign for the abolition of the poll tax should remind us that impotence is an illusion. Change is always resisted by those who wish to preserve their privileges, usually by persuading their critics that 'all is for the best in this the best of all possible worlds' – there is no alternative.

The methods available to the powerful for defusing discontent and pressure for a greater distribution of power and wealth are various. It has been traditional to coopt the leaders of popular movements by offering peerages which take them to the heart of the establishment – as has happened to many trade union and labour leaders.

This seduction is not exclusive to the House of Lords. Members of Parliament are equally vulnerable to the appeal of the Palace by the Thames, and for those who actually achieve ministerial office there is the inner secrecy of the Privy Council.

All political leaders, but especially those of the Labour Party, come to terms with the power centres that exist, and end up doing deals that allow marginal criticism but never extend to a fundamental critique of these power centres' existence.

THE DECAY OF BRITAIN

It would be political suicide for a Prime Minister, however critical of scandal in the City of London, to oppose the right of the City and its international financial allies to use the power of financial speculation to determine the value of the currency. To do so would be to challenge the IMF and the world bankers.

And no Prime Minister, however bedevilled by the excesses of the security services, would dare to question their arrogant claim to determine which groups are acceptable and which subversive, and who then use their immense power to sustain the one and harass or destroy the other. The power of the security services is formidable indeed, committed as they are to a bond of lifelong confidentiality to the Crown which encourages members, behind this wall of impenetrable secrecy, to conduct business in a way that takes them beyond the realms of legal conduct.

Similarly although it is permissible for ministers to express concern about the behaviour of certain members of the Royal Family the existence of the Crown itself has never been questioned. So strong is the commitment to the Crown that in certain circumstances, the person of the monarch may be deemed less important than the survival of the monarchy itself, as Edward VIII learned.

This critical restraint has now extended to the European Community. It is permissible for bureaucratic inefficiencies to be commented upon but the place of Britain within that Community is now undiscussable because the City of London and the industrial organisations are determined to uphold the power of a supranational structure over the rights of the ballot box in Britain to threaten their supremacy.

The effect of these restraints on the democratic process is that the political activity deriving from adult universal suffrage is confined to the simpler question of which political team is to occupy the ministerial offices, to flourish red boxes, and to rotate round the cabinet table.

The fossilised nature of the constitution and political system induces in those who resent this system a sense of utter powerlessness and there is a general paralysis of the public will. This analysis of the state of British democracy has been made more urgent by changes in the last decade which have emphasised the powerlessness of the electorate.

The most serious example is the use of the royal prerogative to sign and to attempt to ratify a treaty of European Union which decants the nation state of Britain into a province of a European federation wherein the power structure will be totally different. The assumption that we are a democratically run country (albeit severely limited) will no longer be right, because appointed Commissioners, an independent central bank, common citizenship and foreign and defence policy will make a mockery of polling day as an expression of the rights of popular sovereignty.

Side by side with the attempted transfer of political control to the European Union has been a centralisation of residual powers in Britain in which the advance of technology has made administrative control easier to justify and to enforce.

Computerisation of record-keeping has enabled the interchange of information gathered for separate purposes, information which we are falsely told is still in the interest of the confidentiality of the citizen but which is accessible to the security services.

Tight secrecy and news management have served the executive well as a form of pre-censorship: D-notices to the media; statutory bans like that on Sinn Fein members and the silencing of Peter Wright have worked in parallel with a system of private briefings, news blackouts and propaganda.

Alongside these recent disturbing developments in

Britain a new and pessimistic analysis of the changes by writers and commentators has emerged. The intellectual justification for the political position that there is no alternative neutralises any ideas of improvement or fundamental change. The distinguished American economist J. K. Galbraith has coined the phrase *the culture of contentment* to explain why politics have become so stale, and another American, Francis Fukuyama, has described the period through which we are passing as 'the end of history', thus acting as a jailer who has confined us to our dungeon and thrown away the key.

We are told that the differences of interest between capital and labour, or rich and poor, have become irrelevant and that an indolent, hopeless under-class which has developed consists of those who have failed to come to terms with the post-socialist world.

Although a command economy under a vanguard party which repressed its own dissenters never appealed to those brought up in the British democratic and socialist tradition, the collapse of the communist regimes was used to declare the death of socialism everywhere, symbolised by the fall of the Berlin wall.

In the absence of any thoughtful or fundamental analysis of the crisis which European capitalism was likewise facing, the Labour Party decided that the best hope for it lay in accepting the central tenets of late 20th-century conservative philosophy. The modernisers adopted a posture appropriate for a team of competent managers, who would be waiting to take over from the Conservative Government; in taking this line, they also threw away their analytical and representative role to argue more passionately for those who were failed by the incumbent Government and the system they supported.

This triumphalism of capital reached its peak at the end of the 1980s but did not consider what would happen when the Cold War ended and with it the arguments for high military budgets, the role of NATO etc. For capitalist societies thrived best when confronted by strong communist governments and were able to justify huge sums of public money for arms and new technologies.

But just as communist systems have broken up, the social consensus of capitalist countries is beginning to break up. The consensus reached its peak in the post-war corporatist approach in which capital and labour, having been brought together for the purpose of achieving a military victory, planned the reconstruction of the destroyed European societies. This consensus around tripartism (the government, capital and the trade unions) was appealing, because its method was discussion and cooperation rather than confrontation. Trade unionists and industrialists were given seats at the top tables in and around Whitehall. It worked reasonably well. Full employment made possible the financing of the welfare state and the NHS, a relatively small number of unemployed being carried easily by taxation from the employed. In industry managers and trade unions worked together and developed a tentative first step towards what was interpreted as a more democratic form of industrial management.

These gains were forced upon capital after both the First and Second World Wars, and consolidated under a Labour government, but capitalism never really accepted them as permanent, and was anxious to win back the freedom to run industry and finance in a way that would liberate it from checks by the power of labour and reduce the bureaucratic element of corporatism.

Trade unionism by the Seventies became the scapegoat for the recurrent failures of capitalism and it was alleged against the workers that restrictive practices and exorbitant wage claims were checking Britain's capacity to re-equip and modernise, while high levels of taxation were destroying the initiative of entrepreneurs, managers and the middle classes generally.

It was against this background that the Conservatives, led by Margaret Thatcher, were able to present themselves as the liberators who would break the chains of bureaucracy, high taxation and corporatism, and free the people to participate more independently in the economic miracle that was promised. Interventionist government was to be banished from the land and the magic hand of the market, we were told, would distribute resources more flexibly, more quickly and more skilfully to meet our needs and modernise government and industry.

The arrival of North Sea oil revenues, one of the greatest gifts nature gave this country, made it possible to lubricate these changes and credit was easy to come by, so that working people were induced to borrow more and were told they could be home owners, when in fact they were only allowed to be home buyers with mortgages and other debts.

Now, in the Nineties, the whole perspective for capitalism is changing in a way that few people could have anticipated ten years ago. The liberation and rolling back of frontiers which signalled the end of that consensus has meant in reality a terrible sense of insecurity, anxiety and fear of the consequences of redundancy or unemployment for many people, through absolutely no fault of their own. It is a far cry from the economic miracle of the Eighties.

And while the political leaders agree on such wide areas of policy, from NATO, nuclear weapons, and the desirability of a federal Europe, to the dominance of market forces and the necessity for restraining trade unions, there is no real possibility of a serious assault upon the causes of the crisis.

II

Democratic Rights or Ancient Traditions?

In all cases it must be remembered that a political combination of the lower classes, as such and for their own objects, is an evil of the first magnitude; that a permanent combination of them would make them (now that so many of them have the suffrage) supreme in the country; and that their supremacy, in the state they now are, means the supremacy of ignorance over instruction and of numbers over knowledge.

Walter Bagehot, 1867

The contagion of democracy is great. For a while there has been no course but to let it rage. It has seized hold of many smaller institutions . . . and wrought its havoc there.

Roger Scruton, 1980

Introduction: The Struggle for Rights

There have always been men and women who have cherished ideas of freedom and democracy in the conviction that we are born equal and are entitled to certain guaranteed

14

rights, whether they be natural rights expressed by Thomas Paine, educational rights in Mary Wollstonecraft's *A Vindication of the Rights of Woman,* moral rights in Richard Hooker's theology or rights to the earth's treasury as in the Diggers' works. All have provided a source of inspiration; and the possibility of social transformation suggested by these ideas has fired the dispossessed, encouraging them to rebel against their existing hardships.

But it is only comparatively recently that real progress has been made in the achievement of even basic 'democratic' rights, and in the social and economic sphere rights have never been truly won. Even the development of trade unionism and early socialist reforms have done little more than legalise countervailing powers possessed by working people and extended a degree of common ownership into the realm of public services.

Despite the suffrage gains, the British political system is so steeped in hierarchy that real progress is hindered at every point and the British people are perceived in the late 20th century as quaint subjects of a discredited Crown; and as Britain draws close to the 21st century its people still enjoy no entrenched rights in their constitution, not even the right to vote: only obligations.

This lack of any guaranteed rights is underlined by the subservient status of the British people. The British constitution has entrenched this subservience by describing the people in law as subjects. The term citizen itself was very controversial when, after the French Revolution, the words of the *Marseillaise,* '*Aux armes, Citoyens*', struck terror into the hearts of Edmund Burke and the Tories and Whigs.

Once the concept of rights was recognised in France, the fear of the governing class was that this would inevitably lead to disturbing social changes in Britain, as it did. Three Conservative Secretaries of State resigned in 1867 when the Reform Act, which extended the vote to include a small number of urban working class men, was passed, describing it as 'a political betrayal which has no parallel in our annals'.

Rights and constitutions affect a country's economic, cultural and political life. They grant and set limits to power and its abuse, they define relationships between the individual and the government; and they determine the freedoms a citizen can enjoy. They are the fundamental elements which underlie the objectives of society.

The French constitution embraces 'liberty, equality and fraternity' as rights within the constitution, and the premise of the American constitution is 'life, liberty and the pursuit of happiness'. These two countries may be far from realising these objectives – liberty, equality, fraternity and the pursuit of happiness mean many things to many people – but their presence in the constitution affects the cultural parameters or values by which current practice is judged.

Whatever principles of government or notions of rights are produced within a national culture, if they are to be effective, leaders must either be willing or obliged to implement and respect them.

The constitution of the old USSR established a clear set of governing principles, but there was no mechanism to ensure that it was ruled in accordance with them. The situation in Russia today is not much better as Boris Yeltsin strives with some success to re-invent the constitution to his own advantage. That he may be able to do so is a sign of an imbalanced concentration of political power. The Russian parliament's efforts to compel him to change course depend on what countervailing power they can wield. In the end, when such a conflict of power and interest threatens civil war, the outcome in part depends on who can muster the greatest armed support.

But the ultimate compulsion on the powerful themselves will be the threat of force. Undemocratic government which refuses to respect popular wishes, has many times become the victim of revolution. The English monarchy was forced to concede control of Parliament in 1642 to the aristocracy, and the aristocracy were forced to concede rule of the Americas in 1776. And under the threat of revolutionary overthrow the Western tradition of democratic government has developed.

This tradition of democracy *claims* as its underlying principle the right of people to control the actions of government and hence their own lives and purposes and has usually involved a notion of citizenship – a certain equality of status for all members of a society – and a recognition of the political, civil and social rights people need for that status to be realised, a status which the British constitution does not however acknowledge.

The case for leaving the British Constitution to 'evolve naturally' over the centuries has been unchallenged for too long. The arguments for a written constitution are widespread and have been accepted in most modern democracies, and have a special relevance today arising from the immense extension of state power and the danger of its growing abuse.

The present system in Britain, built upon the historical role of the monarchy, is geared to a strong executive, and its democratic elements are, as it were, accepted on sufferance by the governing class. A 'Grace and Favour' democracy is fragile, easily thrust aside while the legal precedents sustain a strong and unchallengeable executive.

The Commonwealth of Britain Bill contains many safeguards devolving much greater power to subsidiary elements, which would be democratically accountable, thus introducing checks and balances that simply do not exist under the present system. This written constitution allows us to consider how we are to be governed and on what principles.

There is no single undisputed doctrine or theory of democracy and rights. Democracy has been interpreted in different ways in different countries and at different points in history. It is because there is no objective or final definition of democracy and rights that they should be open to reform. A constitution can only be judged as worthwhile by the people who use it at any time.

Tom Paine recognised the need for flexibility when he wrote that:

> Every age and generation must be free to act for itself, in all cases, as the ages and generations which preceded it. . . . Man has no property in man; neither has any generation a property in the generations which are to follow.

The nature, form and content of rights must remain open to alteration by popular agreement. France has had twelve different constitutional arrangements since 1789, each establishing different relationships between people and government. The American constitution has sixteen amendments added to the original ten which formed the 1791 Bill of Rights, the last of which was added in 1971.

Where reform does not occur explicitly, it can arise through creative interpretation.

In recent years the right to abortion in America has been derived from the Fourteenth Amendment to the US Constitution, which says that 'No state shall make or enforce any law which shall abridge the privileges or immunities of citizens of the United States; nor shall any state deprive any person of life, liberty or property without the due process of law.'

The Amendment makes no explicit reference to abortion rights, but the pressure from the pro-abortion lobby was so strong in the early 1970s that in 1973 the Supreme Court chose to create a right to abortion from a loose reading of the general principles of the Amendment. The ruling was always regarded as tenuous, and after a long period of

18

conservative government in the 1980s, the Supreme Court reversed the earlier decision.

Flexibility in constitutional arrangements should be a virtue in any constitution where people wish to avoid entrenching the prejudice, values and privileges of any particular age. The difficulty which is raised by the American experience with abortion, and in many other cases, is that there must be a clear set of rules governing flexibility: change should not be able to be brought about at the whim of the powerful, but should respond to changes in public opinion over what the country's values and objectives should be.

Britain's peculiarly flexible, unwritten and obscure arrangements have allowed reform to be determined by the needs of the powerful, and not the needs of the people. This obscurity is evident in the total lack of entrenched rights, but also in the poorly defined relationship between Parliament and the courts. This results in some confusion over the basis on which the courts can choose to interpret existing law with the effect that, while the law remains on the statute book, such a creative interpretation can limit specific actions of government.

It is because of the peculiar historical development which led to Parliament itself being a High Court, that there is an area of uncertain jurisdiction between Parliament and the courts, both of which are protected by their respective privileges. Thus judges, including magistrates, are appointed by the Lord Chancellor (using the Crown prerogative) but it takes drastic parliamentary action to remove them. And hence the occasional embarrassing paradox for governments that a judicial decision (eg on Government pit closures) will come up with a decision unfavourable to the government.

This mutual distancing between Parliament and the courts has long been accepted in practice, although the courts are required to uphold the laws passed by Parliament and the government is expected to obey the laws as interpreted by the courts, though it can change them.

Those in Britain who advocate a Bill of Rights often argue that they wish to transfer the power to uphold any entrenched rights from Parliament to the judiciary, specifically to limit the scope of action of a government.

Such a move would inevitably politicise judges, and if courts were given the last word on a Bill of Rights this would have the effect of limiting popular change. Instead it would entrench the status quo as the legitimate benchmark. And whereas mass political campaigns have forced the House of Commons to reverse some unpopular laws, few changes have come from the courts, which compared to the US Supreme Court have, with some notable exceptions, been conservative in their approach.

The interpretation of rights must, ultimately, remain in the hands of an elected assembly and be open to reform – simply because there will always be arguments about what 'rights' should be.

Such rights which have become accepted, have not been the gift of monarchs or wise 'governments by the few', or even the outcome of the contemplation of theories of justice and freedom. They are the result of demands by individuals or groups who have the power to press their case.

For those within or with access to government or to wealth it has generally been easy to gain concessions and recognition from the political system. The vote itself was first given to those with property and wealth, because their resources and consent were important to the monarch or government. But historically, those without wealth have had to rely on collective action for their influence and strength.

The idea of collective action, repudiated by the individualistic rhetoric of the 1980s, is simple; collectivity is the circumstance forced on the poor by their poverty. It is only by combining that those without money ever have and ever can achieve improvement to their condition. Individuals who own companies, farmland estates or newspapers can wield great influence by paying people to defend their interests. But without the personal resources which secure that degree of freedom and influence, individuals must join with others to do so.

Of course, democratic advances and rights are inevitably a compromise between that collective struggle, historical circumstance and the class politics existing at the time. For example, before the Second Reform Act, the electorate consisted of about one million men, all of whom qualified to vote on the basis of their ownership of property. The campaigns of the Chartists between 1832 and 1848 maintained a pressure for political reform of a radical nature including universal male suffrage. This pressure was revitalised after the American Civil War and augmented by middle class reform associations. The outcome was legislation between 1867-9 which extended the vote to two million urban working class and middle class men. But the Act's actual contents and timing were the product of Disraeli's 'leap in the dark', a daring attempt to harness what he believed to be a natural deference in the urban working class to ailing aristocratic landowning interests in a Tory Party split over free trade. The reform was not *designed* with the purpose of embracing either an abstract or a popular principle of democracy or citizenship.

In the 20th century the 1911 Act removed the right of that same unelected class in the Lords to have an absolute veto on legislation passed in the House of Commons. But again the Act was not the child of an abstract commitment to democracy. It was the product of the difficulties faced by Lloyd George and the Liberal government in passing a budget against the interests of the aristocracy. Interestingly, though the Preamble of that Act makes clear that the intention was 'to substitute for the House of Lords as at present constituted a second chamber constituted on a popular basis', the Lords has never, of course, been replaced by a democratically elected chamber.

We do not have in Britain a single coherent set of organising principles. Instead in the past 60 years the notion of rights has developed piecemeal as a result of economic and political pressure on the state – a combination of progressive demands and capitalism's need for a healthy and basically educated workforce. William Beveridge, a Liberal, recognised this long before the Second World War.

In consequence, some social rights were recognised in the welfare state (though with questionable success), in the comprehensive school system, the health service and in public housing. Economic rights have been expanded from the protection of rights to private property, to include safeguards against unfair dismissal, to adequate redundancy pay, to statutory sick pay, to a maximum working week, to minimum pay and conditions, to statutory holidays and to collective provision of benefits for those out of work and pensions for the elderly.

There are many instances where the promise contained in the wording of rights has been denied or limited in practice.

In particular the struggle between the right of labour to combine and the need for capitalism to be unfettered has moved backward and forward over the past 200 years as those with wealth and power have tried to protect their privileges in the path of pressure from below.

William Pitt's Combination Acts of 1799 and judicial rulings such as the Taff Vale Judgment of 1901 both had the effect of severely limiting trade union activity. In the latter the House of Lords ruled that trade unions could be held liable for losses of an employer from industrial action. It was against this background that the Labour Party developed, to oppose the anti-working class discrimination. The Osborne Judgement in the House of Lords in 1909 then ruled that it was against the law for unions to be *involved* in political activity, a blatant attempt to kill off the emerging political movement; in particular, the ruling forbade the funding of political parties, *i.e.* the Labour Party, which was planned to represent the interests of collectively organised workers in Parliament, while leaving industry and the aristocratic interest free to fund their own political parties. Pressure on Parliament achieved a change in the law to overturn the ruling of the House of Lords, and the 1913 Trade Union Act restored the right of trade unions to engage in political activity.

The process of trying to curb the rights of trade unions, *i.e.* the power of labour, has continued to the present day, the most obvious recent case being the removal of any right to free association in cases declared by government to be in contravention of 'the national interest'. This was established in court rulings over the Government communications centre, GCHQ. Here the Conservative Government issued an order forbidding staff at GCHQ from being members of a trade union and removing a number of statutory employment rights. The House of Lords supported the Government.

During the 1980s, Britain witnessed a reaction against many respected social, democratic and economic rights by a governing class confident of its ability to act beyond conventional constraints. This was Britain's flexible constitution in action.

The decade saw successive Conservative governments institute a wide range of undemocratic measures.

The abolition of the Greater London Council was carried out 'in the best interests of London and Londoners'.

Protection from unfair dismissal at work during the first two years of employment was removed. Many of the rights of trade unions were eroded. Strip searches against women at Greenham Common accused of a breach of the peace (for surrounding a nuclear base with enough atomic material in it to destroy the human race) were implemented. Members of CND, Liberty and trade unions were tapped and bugged by MI5.

Rights were extensively withdrawn in Northern Ireland, including the right to silence, and the right to broadcast interviews in support of the Republican movement (such pressures including governmental efforts to ban interviews with Senator Ted Kennedy and Ken Livingstone on the subject of Ireland). The right to reinstatement after pregnancy was removed for women working for small businesses. Wages inspectors were cut by 60 per cent, currently allowing 30 per cent of firms to pay wages below the legal minimum set by the wages councils. Wages councils themselves were gradually removed, opening the way for employers to pay sweat-shop wages. The right to equal pay for men and women failed to be implemented and differentials were higher than at any time since the Equal Pay Act of 1975.

Injunctions have been issued to prevent publication of sensitive and incriminating material such as appeared in *Spycatcher*. A senior civil servant, Clive Ponting, was taken to court for revealing secret documents embarrassing to the Government about the sinking of the Argentinian ship the *Belgrano* during the Falklands War, even though he had made them available not to a foreign government, but to the British public.

And on top of this, sixteen million people lost their right to legal aid – there may be a right to due process before the law, but there is no right of access to legal redress.

The British constitution is in a state of permanent

reform. But its development is shaped not so much by principle but by parliamentary pragmatism and practice, and has its roots in a system of government created as a baronial court to King John in 1265. It therefore retains many feudal elements which are quite foreign to democratic tradition. In fact, the British political system suffers rather than enshrines democracy and our rights are defined negatively as being the areas of action not forbidden by law.

In reality, our constitution is an untidy and developing collection of compromises, the consequence of sullen responses to pressure; pressure which reflects the relative strength of wealth versus collective action at different periods of history. When powerful and undemocratic groups are forced to retreat, they wait for the time when they can regain their supremacy.

The superiority of our constitutional methods is illusory. Parliaments and legislatures in other democracies bear little resemblance to our own, often with different conceptions of rights and procedures resulting from different traditions of democracy. Those systems closest to our own were spawned in areas of the globe following periods of British colonial administrations, imposed without the consent of the indigenous populations. The right to self-determination was never applied to the peoples of the British empire. The 'Mother of Parliaments' was in existence throughout all of the years of colonial rule, responsible for the denial of rights. The Indian leader, Gandhi, who had been arrested by the British colonial power, was ridiculed by Churchill who described him on his arrival at independence negotiations in New Delhi as the 'half-naked fakir loping up the steps of the Vice-regal lodge to parley on equal terms with the representative of the King Emperor'. Gandhi, who had many friends in Britain, was asked on a visit to London in 1931 for the Round Table Conference on India, what he thought of civilisation in Britain, and responded, 'I think it would be a very good idea!'

Arguments against democracy

What is needed is a radical reform of the British constitution establishing democratic accountability over those in power and democratic choice over the rights, principles and objectives which they will be obliged to protect and pursue.

Throughout history objections have been raised to the simple principle of democracy on the grounds that 'the people' are incapable of taking important decisions, that government should be left to the elite, the experts, the technocrats.

Edmund Burke referred to the populace as the 'swinish multitude', and a century later Walter Bagehot, the author of the once definitive text on the British Constitution, warned that 'vox populi would be vox diaboli', if suffrage was extended to minor English shop-keepers.

Such objections conceal a range of powerful vested interests. They are an extension of the 'good king' aspect of British political culture that the people at the very top are so rich and powerful and wise that they are incorruptible – the Whig and Tory principle.

The surviving aristocratic element of modern Britain is the somewhat precarious peak of a pyramid of seniority and social rank, at the base of which is the labourer, and the top of which is the monarch with a multitude of ranks between the two.

Through life we are expected to obey authority and are persuaded to believe that our 'betters' *are* actually better and know what is good for us. Education and work are organised around the notion of failure, the fate of the majority. The success of the few, via further education, funded by the state, relies on the rejection of the many.

Deference at work and bowing and scraping are a part of most people's life experience, an experience which excludes any idea that there might be a better or fairer way of structuring our social relations.

In the 1960s Prince Charles, then a schoolboy at Gordonstoun, concluded from his history books that: 'By entrusting the management of affairs chiefly to the upper classes a country is at least saved from some of the evil that may be produced in the lower classes by corruption. Although the upper classes may be lacking intelligence, biased by class interest and guilty of great corruption in political appointment, the honour of the class at least secures it from the greater corruption when its members are permanently connected with the well-being of the country.' Presumably no master dared to correct him.

The view that the best government must be government of the few, has a long history and remains an important part of modern British psychology. Prince Charles was reinterpreting Burke, who wrote 200 years earlier that the 'occupation of an hair-dresser, or of a working tallow-chandler, cannot be a matter of honour to any person – to say nothing of a number of other more servile employments . . . The state suffers oppression, if such as they, either individually or collectively, are permitted to rule.'

The intellectual and cultural superiority of 'the higher classes' is used to justify the exclusion of the vast majority of people from influencing the hand of government. The rule of reason and principle, proven by tradition, should exclude the uneducated masses from power. Kenneth Minogue at the London School of Economics continues the tradition. 'Conservatives', he says, 'regard ruling as a special kind of skill, possibly arcane and certainly not universally distributed among members of the human race. It is learned by practice and example and therefore is likely to be most highly developed among members of a long established ruling class.'

The tradition of superiority based either on the virtues of the aristocracy or on special knowledge and expertise is recycled by academics and commentators.

For the aristocratic tradition, virtue stems supposedly from the disinterested nature of that class which is 'above politics'. This tradition is in contrast to the corruption and self-interest of business and 'trade' (or trade unionism). Thus the growth of a new commercial ethos has been seen as breaking with some rosy past. Jeremy Paxman in his book on the British establishment, *Friends in High Places*, repeats the lament made by Trollope over a century earlier in *The Way We Live Now* about the decline of aristocratic virtues. Ironically, Paxman sees this as weakening British democracy:

> The tension between the old and the new orders reveals how much British public life depended upon gentlemen's agreements: there were some things gentlemen just didn't do. The erosion of those values has strengthened the case for statutory edifices to protect basic freedoms like a Bill of Rights.

The aristocratic tradition – into which the rich and the clever are coopted by peerages – with its interests protected by unity, continuity and stability, still conceives the workings of a modern democracy as factional, reforming, and unstable.

The technocratic tradition by contrast is modern in outlook and offers a radical break with the past. Government can be operated through expertise, and society broken down into specialised functional units, governed by a system of rational management. The early Fabians, Sidney and Beatrice Webb, admired a technocratic administration of society along the lines developed in the Soviet state: not so much socialism as a sort of paternalism by civil servants and experts. The problems of government could, they believed, be solved by a rational discussion of ends among experts.

In its modern form, the tradition envisages a tidy separation of party politics and government from the specialised functions of the economy with an independent central bank, and management by industrialists, financiers and consultants. Politics becomes a specialisation in its own right. Government becomes a process of administration, staffed by professionals, and though an element of popular accountability may be prudent, politicians are guided by advisers rather than their electorate. Political choices become the preserve of pundits, opinion researchers, and think-tank reports. Economic choices are judged feasible or otherwise by consultation with self-appointed oracles in the City.

In both traditions, the people themselves are regarded as suspect – either corrupt, ignorant or uninterested – and as the recipients or consumers of government policy rather than as citizens to whom government should be accountable.

Elites will invariably rule in their own interest, persuading themselves and others of the objectivity of their case for leadership and the inevitability of their position of power. Cabinet ministers, civil servants, university professors, think-tank chiefs, leading journalists, newspaper editors, economists, and financial advisors could conceivably all be right. Expert advice may frequently be useful. But in a democracy, that judgement should be left to those who are affected by expert rule – those who have to live with the outcome of the duties, rights and privileges it seeks to establish.

The British people have acquiesced to many pronouncements from leading politicians and experts which were never true, and should never have been accepted. Leaders do not have a monopoly on competence, but they enjoy a substantial monopoly over the power to control the underlying nature of life in British society – to create security or insecurity, to protect the weakest or to liberate the fittest, to meet the needs of profit or the needs of people themselves. Choices such as these are of great importance. In spite of declarations to the contrary that 'historical progress is dead', or that 'what we have is the best we can hope for', there is no reason why people should regard the society in which they live as the pinnacle of human achievement. If popular will is strong enough, important choices can still be made which will allow people to improve the condition of their lives. But they can only be made if the institutions of government are compelled to respond to democratic pressures.

Not only should people be free to campaign for enforceable rights which governments will then adhere to, but in addition the choice of rights, which includes the democratic rights established by the constitution, should be left to the people whom they will affect. This choice is not a final one. Rights need to be continually reassessed. New campaigns, new issues and new ideas will gather support while others decline. Furthermore, there has to be some guarantee that those empowered to implement or uphold any particular system of rights, actually do so in practice. It is governments and the courts which implement rights and there must be some method for ensuring that they are held accountable to the people whom their power affects. If they are not, then there is no guarantee that rights which have formally been recognised will be effective or respected in practice.

The importance of tradition

Britain's government owes more to the aristocratic and technocratic traditions than to any other. We have inherited a hierarchical system of government dominated by the ethos of the Crown. Reforms over the years have left relatively untouched a number of constitutional devices which, originally designed to empower the monarch, can be used by the Prime Minister and senior cabinet ministers to distance the actions of government from accountability to the electorate.

The power of democracy is that it enforces accountability, and can replace those found wanting. An undemocratic political system has accountability too, but the governors are accountable to those *above* them and allegiance flows up the social hierarchy. It is this which distinguishes government in the spirit of the good king from government in the spirit of democracy.

But the chain of democratic accountability in Britain is very weak. The House of Commons is a very imperfect legislature. The government can dominate it with relative ease: individual MPs have inadequate resources to counter government power even if they wanted to, the hours are difficult, it is unrepresentative of the majority of the population, and the business is too great to allow proper scrutiny of the administration. The Prime Ministerial system of government has been described as an 'elective dictatorship'. In reality, the power of government is severely limited, though not by the electorate: the House of Commons is only one of several groups or, for lack of a better term, institutions, whose support the Prime Minister will require to retain power and govern 'successfully'.

Members of Parliament and members of powerful institutions may believe they sustain a democracy. But the political system they inhabit embodies the idea of government by the wise expert. The nature of the British constitution not only isolates the executive powers under Crown Prerogatives from control by the House of Commons, but also engenders conservatism and superiority within the governing classes.

This superiority is derived directly from the Crown, which is both the fountain of all honour and the source of much power and which provides a means for securing the loyalty of bureaucrats, the military and secret services as servants of the nation rather than the people. The Crown is the keystone in the arch of the state. The authority of tradition serves to strengthen the pillars of hierarchy and privilege on which the Crown rests and to divert attention from the absurdity of a hereditary head of state. Each part of the architecture must be preserved to protect the whole. Anyone bold enough to challenge the tradition of heredity in the Lords, for example, is accused of undermining the Crown. The Lords must remain intact because without it the monarchy would be threatened and that would threaten the British way of life itself. It is a symbiotic dependence – the Crown and the House of Lords protect each other.

This argument was used in the early 1960s to fend off the challenge to the hereditary principle presented by peers wishing to renounce their titles. A peerage was an *incorporeal hereditament* fixed in the blood. To allow renunciation of an hereditary peerage was, according to one Conservative MP, to 'forget the important benefits which this country derives from the maintenance of the hereditary principle. The Queen is only accepted by all the Commonwealth countries as their head because she inherits her position. No elected head of state could possibly hope to maintain the confidence of all the Commonwealth countries. In tampering with the hereditary principle we must beware that we do not set on foot a process which would end with the abolition of the Monarchy itself.'

The same argument had been used much earlier during the proposed extension of the franchise in 1831. Sir Robert Peel, opposing the Reform Bill, said: 'I am convinced that it is not founded on the acknowledged principles of the constitution – because it does not give security to the prerogative of the Crown – because it does not guarantee the legitimate rights, influences and privileges of both Houses of Parliament.'

Disestablishment of the Church of England, of which the Queen is supreme governor, is rejected for the same reasons. The separation of the church from the state threatens the monarchy. But the existence of the Crown protects the archbishops and the bishops in the House of Lords and legitimizes the power of the state over almost all church appointments from top to bottom.

In recent debates over membership of the European Community it has been argued by some who wish to defend their own interests that closer union within Europe threatens the permanence of the monarchy. The threat to the institution of the Crown is quite real. Membership of a full European Union makes the Queen a citizen of Europe, with the same rights and privileges as her subjects. If resident abroad she would be able to vote in local elections in other countries, something she has never been able to do in her own kingdom. European Union imposes a competing source of authority in the shape of Brussels, which is a great danger to those who rely on the Crown rather than the European Community for their power and status.

Nevertheless, the strength of the Crown should not be underestimated. It holds in its power considerable rewards which reinforce a culture of subservience undermining and opposing a culture of democratic accountability under which we elect, support and maintain our representatives.

There is no greater illustration of the power of deference than when, after his abdication as Edward VIII, the Duke of Windsor, in an interview with the TUC-run *Labour Herald*, offered himself as President of a Republic should a Labour Government want to introduce one. The TUC, however, refused to print the story for fear that it would be thought to be republican.

Arguments against reform

Tradition has been used to block full scale constitutional reform.

33

People speak of our unwritten constitution's flexibility and ability to survive through the centuries as a virtue but its continuity, which is the preservation of the powers of the Crown from democratic control, is precisely its weakness.

The British people are urged not to destroy a system which is said to have evolved to fit the needs of British society. According to John Patten, 'we turn against grand designs and build on what has worked; on what has been built up generation by generation by our people of all Parties in all Parliaments.' The constitution is the embodiment of the wisdom of parliaments throughout the ages which outweighs the impertinent claims of any one generation. Because the constitution has lasted, it is argued it has value.

But evolution of a constitution does not imply that it is the best, merely that the system which has evolved has best fitted its environment. An environment where power has been given to privilege and hierarchy, will, over a period of time, have favoured certain outcomes over others, and will undoubtedly have protected those aspects of the constitution which favoured established or powerful interests. Sometimes the process of change will have worked in the interests of democracy, but will only have done so when popular pressure has combined with the willingness of established elites to allow reform.

Even so, the present system with all its faults, the traditionalists argue, should be preserved from change because it continues to enjoy the consent of the people. But passivity does not imply consent and never has done. An increasing number of people now harbour a deep and growing cynicism about politics and politicians. The Government's complacency and lack of responsiveness has caused people to retreat reluctantly from political remedies, and to switch where they are wealthy enough to do so to individualistic ones – private health insurance, private housing, private education – with all the uncertainty and cost that involves, and with the outcome that a large number are far worse off.

This resignation and pessimism should not be mistaken for a welcoming endorsement of the status quo. People might accept things they never should, simply because they are encouraged to lack the confidence and hope that something can be done.

Collective solutions designed to meet society's needs failed to live up to expectations, but people must examine how far the blame rests with the political system which created local government, welfare services, and nationalised industries in its own hierarchical, centralised and unresponsive image.

It is the nature of political institutions and not the nature of collective provision which has contributed to Britain's decline; what is needed is a new constitution which allows people to create their own solutions and define their own living conditions and removes the power from elites to do things for them. Professor Philip Norton, a writer on constitutional theory and opponent of reform, believes that 'The busy housewife concerned with getting in the weekly groceries has no time to waste on such questions. To the young unemployed black in Liverpool the questions are incomprehensible.'

To the busy housewife and the young unemployed black why their situation exists is incomprehensible.

III
How Democratic is Britain?

What is this metaphor called a Crown, or rather what is monarchy? Is it a thing, or is it a name, or is it a fraud. Is it a 'contrivance of human wisdom' or of human craft to obtain money from a nation under specious pretences. Is it a thing necessary to a nation?

Tom Paine, 1791

All the rights and duties of the British people stem from the powers of the Crown. The legal authority of the state is the monarch. Thus, defendants in court are prosecuted by *the Crown* and not *the people*. This is a surface reflection of a deeper reality; that the executive powers of the state – the powers to sign treaties, make state appointments and go to war – do not derive from a democratic constitution, but are the prerogative powers of the Crown.

The mythology and magic surrounding the Crown and the Royal Family have always been used both to entrench this culture of deference and to veil a whole range of undemocratic powers protected by the concept 'royal prerogatives'. It is a potent combination.

The royal prerogative has its roots in the oath taken by William the Conqueror. When he crowned himself in Westminster Abbey on Christmas Day, 1066, he vowed 'before the altar of Peter the Apostle, and in the presence of the clergy and the people, to defend the holy churches of God and their Governors, *to rule over the whole people subject to me*, justly and with Royal Provenance, to enact and preserve rightful laws, and strictly to forbid violence and unjust judgements'.

The prerogatives represent a formidable array of legal powers. The nationalisation of the Church of England was effected by royal prerogative, the establishment of the Royal Mail in 1660 by Charles II was by royal prerogative.

The powers have been moderated by and modified by the influence of the Commonwealth period (1649–60) and the Glorious Revolution of 1688, when Parliament allegedly invited William and Mary to replace James II, and the prerogatives have been restricted by statute from time to time. Many have been ceded to the control of the government. But whether in the possession of the government or the monarch, they remain immense in scope and supersede many of the powers of the elected Commons.

Certain executive powers are always vested in the head of state, as such powers normally derive either from the written constitution of a country or from statute passed by Parliament.

Not so the British Crown, which can in law dissolve Parliament, ask an individual to form a government, declare war, sign treaties, make ministers, create peers, appoint archbishops, bishops and judges, grant pardons or issue commissions without consulting Parliament at all. All but the first two powers are actually exercised by and with the advice of the Prime Minister, and, in theory any Prime

Minister could be brought down in the Commons if the powers were grossly abused. One important prerogative is the right to go to war without consulting Parliament. The House of Commons has no legal right to be consulted. The Falklands and Gulf Wars were never put to the vote for decision.

Treaty making has acquired enormous importance and again treaties do not have to be confirmed by the Commons. The government in Britain can enter treaties openly or secretly: the NATO treaty being an open one, the agreement to US bases in Britain a secret one. This power has acquired a new and greater importance since 1973, when Britain joined the then Common Market, because the signature to the Treaty of Accession was given under royal prerogative: and when Prime Minister Edward Heath signed it, the text had not even been published. Likewise, although the Government declined to use the royal prerogative in the event, it could have done so to ratify the Treaty of Maastricht in 1993, and bypass Parliament.

The most useful prerogative of the Prime Minister is the power of patronage exercised by him or her: the appointment and dismissal of ministers; the appointment of peers, archbishops and bishops; and an extensive system of honours and titles. It takes 43 million electors to elect 651 MPs, but took only ten Prime Ministers, from Attlee to Major, to make 840 peers.

When too many powers are vested in the person of the Prime Minister, voters are voting for a multiplicity of interests. Democracy should not be about the appointment and dismissal of, in Hailsham's words, an 'elected dictator' but about accountability throughout the period of a government.

The powers to dissolve and to invite an individual to form a government are formidable in theory and could also be in practice. If the Prime Minister had a majority but the establishment wanted for some reason to get rid of him or her it would be open to the Crown, in the person of the Queen, to dissolve Parliament. That is her personal prerogative. The dismissal of Gough Whitlam, the Australian Prime Minister by Governor-General Kerr in 1975 was the last example of that power being used, and although the Palace disclaimed any responsibility for the decision itself it was taken under the devolved prerogatives which came from the Crown.

Circumstances might arise whereby a government had been popularly elected, but against it was a lot of international pressure, the polls were beginning to turn, the City was very discontented, and the Crown decided to intervene. The Prime Minister could find him or herself removed and could do nothing about it. No British monarch would dare to do such a thing, if there was a risk of the person thus dismissed being re-elected in the general election that would follow. Such an act would bring about a crisis in the relations with a freshly-elected government and that could lead to a reaction against the Crown in favour of a republic. But a well-timed dissolution at a moment when a government was unpopular would not be so difficult to engineer. The courts would have to uphold such an act under the powers of the Crown, and any Prime Minister displaced in that way who appealed to the judges (all of whom owe allegiance to the Crown personally) to declare the dissolution illegal would be told that his or her power to head the administration had been removed quite legally.

For the same reason the *personal power of the Crown* to grant or refuse a Prime Minister a dissolution if he or she requests one is also of the greatest significance. In refusing one, the Crown could obstruct a government that wished to take an issue to the people, as Edward Heath did over the coal strike in early 1974. If the Crown had refused that request, Heath would have had to fight out the battle with the miners with the public against him, and this might well have had a profound influence upon the balance of political power in this country.

The obverse of this power of dissolution personal to the sovereign is the power to decide whom to ask to form a government. In the past the Crown did have the deciding word on the choice of Prime Minister. Until 1965 the Conservative Party leader 'emerged' after mysterious consultations and the Crown was advised by various people as to whom it might call. When Bonar Law was retiring on health grounds in 1923, Lord Curzon was expecting to be appointed, but King George V was advised that it was no longer suitable to have the Prime Minister sitting in the Lords, and Baldwin was chosen. In more recent years, in an ironic twist, Lord Home emerged from the Lowlands of Scotland to succeed Macmillan after Rab Butler had been considered and rejected by the charmed circle. Home then had to divest himself of his peerage and be found a Commons seat.

In circumstances of a hung Parliament the question of whom the monarch should invite to form a government becomes enormously important. Suppose after a general election all three main parties had the same number of seats. The monarch could call any one of the three with equal legitimacy but each one would require an alliance with one of the others. A Prime Minister, thus chosen, could begin a period as PM, move into No 10, make announcements and appoint a cabinet, so gaining an unfair but all-important advantage before the new Parliament met.

If a Prime Minister of a minority government could not get his or her legislation through Parliament, he or she could apply to the Queen for a dissolution to hold another election. But the Queen *could* refuse and the Prime Minister would then resign and she would have to summon someone else. The granting or withholding of such power is potentially very great.

The limiting factor in the exercise of the royal prerogative is fear by the monarch or royal advisers of making a mistake. Supposing the Queen had refused Heath a dissolution in February 1974: he would have been in conflict with the monarch. Alternatively, if the Queen had dissolved Parliament against the wishes of a Prime Minister, and the same Prime Minister had won the election, there would be a constitutional crisis.

For these reasons, the Crown might very well wish to rid itself of this power.

These are by no means imaginary circumstances to contemplate. The only limitation at present upon the effective use of such personal prerogatives would be the extent to which the royal advisers felt it wise to use them, bearing in mind that the survival of the Crown will always be their prime concern.

If a particular monarch became an embarrassment to the British establishment, that person would be removed, as James II was and replaced by a stronger, Protestant king. Likewise when Edward VIII visited the Rhondda Valley in 1936, witnessed the terrible unemployment there and said 'Something must be done', that alarmed the establishment, and when he subsequently persisted in his marriage plans to an 'unsuitable' woman, Baldwin threatened him with the resignation of the government. After consultation throughout the empire, the British establishment decided that they would rather force the monarch to abdicate than allow him to marry a divorced woman.

Oaths – the real constitution

Underpinning the constitutional arrangements of the Crown is a hidden written constitution – the network of ancient tribal oaths of allegiance to the Crown. Everyone with British nationality is a subject of the Crown bound by a personal obligation of loyalty to the monarch. The betrayal of that duty, can, in certain circumstances, constitute the offence of High Treason, attracting the death penalty.

Over and above any general duty as subjects, all those who hold positions of responsibility within the state are required to swear an oath*, or make a solemn affirmation, of allegiance to the Queen personally, and to her heirs and successors.

This oath is imposed upon all Members of Parliament and peers, and is a pre-condition of their right to take their seats in Parliament. Gerry Adams, who as a Republican MP was not willing to swear that oath, could not take his seat in the House of Commons, even though he had been elected a Republican and for a political allegiance which was openly canvassed.

Adams's election was thus effectively cancelled out by the Crown. Had he attempted to take his seat without swearing the oath he would have been guilty of a serious offence and subject to a heavy fine.

One hundred and seventy years ago, no Roman Catholic could be admitted to the Commons. The oath of allegiance established by an Act of the Scottish Parliament of 29 August, 1681 to secure *'the protestant religion against Papists and Phanaticks'* required the people to *'bear Faith and true Allegiance to the King's Majesty, His Heirs and Lawful Successors'*.

* See Appendix 3

It also states the claim of the established church –
nationalised by Henry VIII – to be the sole interpretation of
the Word of God. The people must swear, it said in 1681,
'*That [they] Allow and sincerely Profess the True Protestant
Religion*' and '*believe the same to be founded on and agreeable
unto the Written Word of God; And [they] Promise and Swear,
That [they] shall Adhere thereto all the dayes of [their]
Life-time; And shall endeavour to Educate [their] Children
therein.*'

Though the modern oath is worded differently, it seems
preposterous to have a single orthodoxy of this kind
enforced as a test of loyalty to the Crown. And yet the
position is very little changed. The Church of England
remains the established state religion. The oath of allegiance still exists, though requiring that those in authority
swear to '*be faithful and bear true allegiance to Her Majesty
Queen Elizabeth, her heirs and successors, according to law*'.

There remains an implicit oath of religious allegiance
since the Queen, in her coronation oath swears '*to the utmost
of [her] power [to] maintain and preserve inviolably the
settlement of the Church of England, . . . [and to] preserve
unto the Bishops and Clergy of England, and to the Churches
there committed to their charge, all such rights and privileges, as
by law do or shall appertain to them or any of them.*'

So the constitutional obligations of the monarch are to
preserve the power and privileges of the established church,
one particular religious denomination among many within
Britain, while the rights of the people are nowhere mentioned within the oath. In return the bishops are required to
make a homage to the Queen recognising that she is '*the
only supreme governor of this realm in spiritual and ecclesiastical things as well as in temporal*'.

One particular religious tradition has been cemented into
our constitutional arrangements, while democratic rights
are absent.

Cabinet ministers are required to take a second oath to the MPs' oath, in their capacity as members of the Privy Council. The Privy Councillors' oath requires no affirmation or consent. It is read out to an incoming Minister and is thereby 'administered', and the administration of an oath is precisely that, like an injection. The wording of the oath, for years an official secret, was drawn up long before universal adult suffrage and Parliamentary democracy. It imposes upon cabinet ministers the duty that they will to their *uttermost bear Faith and Allegiance unto the Queen's Majesty; and will assist and defend all Jurisdictions, Pre-eminences, and Authorities, granted to her Majesty . . . .And generally in all things [they] will do as a faithful and true Servant ought to do to Her Majesty.'*

The potential legal effect of these oaths is very serious. In certain circumstances these oaths would be enforced by the courts, in the same way that the courts have been used to enforce the duty of life-long confidentiality owed to the Crown, as became apparent during the *Spycatcher* case. According to the Radcliffe Report on ministerial memoirs of 1975, it is the Privy Councillor oath that places retiring cabinet ministers 'under an obligation to protect official information entrusted to them' even from the people by whom they were elected and to whom they are accountable, *i.e.* ex-cabinet ministers cannot in theory reveal in retrospect discussion or decisions made by elected governments.

While in other modern democracies, the President, as head of state, takes an oath to uphold the constitution, the oaths of allegiance in Britain contain no obligation to serve the interests of the people or to respect democratic rights. The governing principles of the constitution remain centralising and hierarchical, dividing those in power from those who elect them.

Indeed, in this country the nature of democracy is hardly discussed at all. We are taught 'government' as an endorsement of the status quo, not in any analytical way, and when school children visit the House of Commons, they are shown where the Queen sits for the state opening of Parliament, the route the Speaker's procession takes to the Chamber, where the Mace is deposited, etc., but not any of the commemorations of democratic advance – because there aren't any.

In so far as any advance in our democratic arrangements is discussed it is the 'Glorious Revolution' of 1688, which was actually a coup d'état by the Protestant William and Mary of Orange. The period of Cromwell's Commonwealth is commonly referred to by the traditionalists as the inter-regnum – the period between two kings. There are no official memorials in the Commons to the Chartists or the suffragettes or any of those who fought for the vote or opened the Commons to catholics, atheists and Jews.

Prime Ministerial power and accountability

We are told that power has moved over time from the throne to the Lords, from the Lords to the Commons and from the Commons to the people. But in practice power has now moved to the Prime Minister who then, exercising the powers of the Crown without explicit consent from Parliament, dominates the whole system.

A Prime Minister with these constitutional powers is in theory accountable to Parliament, whose support any Prime Minister requires to stay in office. But the Prime Minister is in practice able to use the fact that he or she is leader of a normally disciplined majority party, and in addition controls access to a range of governmental posts and state honours with which to provide a cushion of loyal and generally reliable support in Parliament.

The House of Commons is the only elected part of

Parliament and democratic principles should require that all prerogative powers be controlled by that House.

At present any Prime Minister must depend upon the support of powerful ministers or interest groups both inside and outside Parliament, but reliance on the consent of the governed is minimal. A modern Prime Minister controls government like a feudal monarch, exercising Crown powers but dependent on key interests to support the regime.

Powers of patronage are one weapon at the disposal of the Prime Minister granted by the Crown. The problem of patronage begins long before any honour or government position has been awarded. The influence of patronage extends far beyond the number of people who actually receive an honour or appointment, to those who expect or desire one. For a very large number of people, their position, promotion or honour depends upon the favour of senior ministers, and civil servants who have the ear of the Prime Minister. They would be less than human if this did not in some way affect their conduct.

Hopes of patronage help to cement the loyalty of those in the parliamentary parties who aspire to office in government and opposition. And the threat of dismissal and the ability to reallocate important portfolios ensures that those within government remain loyal to the Prime Minister. Government ministers have to agree to abide by rules of conduct which the Prime Minister issues personally. These rules are laid down in a minute entitled *Questions of Procedure for Ministers* drawn up by the Cabinet Secretariat and issued by each Prime Minister when he or she takes office. These procedure minutes have never been submitted to cabinet for approval, but contain regulations governing everything from a minister's exposure in the media to the use of official cars.

The most important of these rules is the convention of collective responsibility, originally established when the monarch still presided over cabinet, in order to strengthen ministers against the Crown. When the franchise was extended collective responsibility became an instrument for sustaining the cabinet against Parliament and the electorate. If collective responsibility is to protect individual members of government from being picked off one by one, the government must present a united face, take collective responsibility for actions, and then stand or fall together. If Parliament were to defeat the legislation of one minister, it could be held to be a defeat for the cabinet as a whole. If the government were then forced to resign it could cause the dissolution of the Commons, ending the life of the Parliament and jeopardising MPs' seats. The intertwining of the interests of the cabinet with the interests of the legislature gives the government considerable power – the Commons will only use its ability to defeat the government as a last resort. 'Either the executive legislates and acts, or else it can dissolve'. Either the government and its majority in the Commons stand together or they fall together.

The outcome is that government back-benchers, who will generally want to see their party continue in power rather than risk losing all at a general election, can usually be relied upon to fall into line. Back-bench rebellion against governments has therefore been limited. The 1950s and 60s saw very few outbreaks of cross-party voting against a government due to the strict enforcement of party whips. Dissent has increased since the 1970s partly because it has been shown that a government can stand a number of minor defeats and resignations without falling. But it probably remains the case that on an issue that might be a threat to the government, or which might precipitate a vote of confidence, party discipline will be severe and when it really matters, back-benchers will support the government, such as was evidenced in the Conservative Government decision to close large numbers of coal-mines and its back-bench rebels fell into line.

Collective responsibility not only galvanises back-bench support for government, but disciplines rebels and dissenters within government. 'Difficult' ministers can be blocked, or moved to the sidelines by threats of dismissal by the Prime Minister, the removal of responsibility for a specific policy or by letting it be known to the senior civil servants in that department that the minister is out of favour with the Prime Minister. In this situation, civil servants withdraw active cooperation from the minister.

The power to threaten the collective dissolution of Parliament through a Prime Minister's own resignation and a call for an election has in fact never been tested in practice. The present Prime Minister, John Major, was forced to retreat on one motion in Parliament on Maastricht, and when Wilson threatened in 1969 to resign unless the Parliamentary party accepted the White Paper on trade unions, *In Place of Strife*, he was advised that if he tried to dissolve Parliament, the then chairman of the Parliamentary Labour Party would follow him to Buckingham Palace to request that James Callaghan take over. Wilson capitulated and the White Paper was dropped.

However, in certain circumstances the threat of resignation can be effective and votes of confidence within cabinet can succeed where hours of persuasion have failed. An alternative sanction for a Prime Minister will be to threaten the sack, potentially destroying a ministerial career.

In these ways the Prime Minister is able to make personal decisions, in consultation with a few key colleagues, binding on the whole government so that decisions which are not collectively taken must be collectively supported in Parliament and in the press. In Callaghan's *Questions of Procedure* it had already been established that 'Decisions reached by the Cabinet or Cabinet Committees are binding on all members of the government'.

Wilson had previously required that those members had a duty 'not merely to support the Government but to refrain from making any speech or doing any act which may appear to implicate the Government'.

In spite of the assumption that collective cabinet responsibility is a convention of the constitution, it was waived by Wilson in 1975 over the issue of the Referendum on European membership. Later, Callaghan, in a parliamentary answer, made it clear that collective cabinet responsibility applied when he said it did.

When it is in force, collective responsibility does not simply bind cabinet ministers, but applies to all members of the government including Ministers of State, law officers, Under-secretaries of State and the whips, who will be expected to support the decisions of the cabinet, both in Parliament and elsewhere in public. It will also be expected to apply to MPs who serve as parliamentary private secretaries to ministers. In consequence the Prime Minister can expect up to half of his or her parliamentary majority to be guaranteed by virtue of these MPs being members of government, however junior, and therefore on what has been dubbed 'the pay-roll vote'.

A large amount of government business passes through a system of cabinet committees, staffed by ministers appointed by the Prime Minister. At any one time there are likely to be over one hundred ad hoc and standing committees. Through this system difficult ministers can be by-passed and problematic issues can be removed from the agenda of full cabinet, a system used extensively by Margaret Thatcher. According to the 1992 *Questions of Procedure* they buttress 'the principle of collective responsibility by ensuring that, even though an important question may never reach the Cabinet itself . . . the final judgement will be sufficiently authoritative to ensure that the Government as a whole can be properly expected to accept responsibility for it'.

In other words decisions made by a Prime Minister and his or her appointees in cabinet committee have the force of a cabinet decision, even though the issues may never come to cabinet or be discussed with interested ministers. The Prime Minister can even keep the minutes of committees secret from cabinet ministers not present.

Harold Wilson wrote in 1974:

> The fact that no Minister is in practice able to partici-
> pate in the decision-taking process over the whole
> range of Government policy does not alter the position.
> The obligations of collective responsibility are binding
> on all members of the Government, in the sense that it
> is unacceptable for any Minister publicly to dissociate
> himself [sic] from the policies and actions of the
> Government of which he is a member. If he feels
> impelled by reasons of conscience so to dissociate
> himself, he must resign in order to do so. This applies
> to all Ministers; it applies especially to members of the
> Cabinet.

Prime Ministers have a position in cabinet which is very much more than first among equals, and they can ensure that policy is made in highly personalised and secretive form under their own direction. But in spite of the personal character of many of the decisions all members of the government will be expected to support the decisions made in committee.

The civil service and accountability

A further element of personal control of government is given to the Prime Minister by his or her position as head of the civil service. The relationship is not one-way. The senior ranks of the civil service have their own particular agenda and the fact that they hold the key to substantial control of the Whitehall machine gives them a great deal of influence over the Prime Minister.

In parallel with each cabinet committee is an official committee sharing the same title as its ministerial counter-part, but with the suffix (O). The most important of these is the Committee of permanent secretaries known informally in Whitehall as Cabinet (O). Taken together, this network of civil service committees forms the permanent government, and plays an important part in coordinating – and shaping – government policy.

The Prime Minister, as head of the civil service, controls a substantial executive machine. His or her control is exercised quite simply: the Prime Minister appoints and confirms permanent secretaries and has some control over their status and operational conduct. The result is that permanent secretaries within each government department are likely to have greater loyalty to Number 10 than to their own minister. Indeed, civil servants have been known to keep Prime Ministers informed of the activities of ministers who act against their implied wishes. In addition the Cabinet Office has its own extensive research facilities and will prepare briefings and papers for use in cabinet, which support the Prime Minister's position, on any matter, including those which are the specific concern of a cabinet minister.

But while the Prime Minister as head of the civil service commands great power, senior civil servants tend to view governments as visitors to the royal suite at the Grand Hotel and they themselves comprise the real permanent government, regarding their loyalty to a sense of national interest embodied in the Crown. Despite attempts by Margaret Thatcher as Prime Minister to break this inherent resistance to radical policies, through a series of fundamental reforms, the power of the permanent secretaries remains strong. Because of the high degree of centralisation, civil servants are able to maintain a broad continuity in policy between different governments in line with their own judgement of what is best.

Former head of the Civil Service Department (subsequently Cabinet Secretary) Robert Armstrong spoke frankly when he wrote in 1974 that 'it would have been enormously difficult for any minister to change the framework [of policy], so to that extent we had great power'. Adding 'I don't think we used it maliciously or malignly, I think we chose that framework because we thought it the best one going'.

A similar attitude was held by George Young, deputy head of MI6, in 1979. He says quite openly that:

> The higher reaches of the Civil Service undoubtedly make most of the decisions for Ministers and put them in front of them and say 'Minister do you agree?' The ethos of the higher reaches of the Civil Service is not one of stirring up hornets' nests, particularly if some of your best friends are hornets, but in my experience of dealing with Ministers . . . they don't hear what you say; you tell them something, it goes in one ear and it's out of the other and they're busy thinking up the next Parliamentary answer to the next Parliamentary question.

The present constitutional arrangements are such that elected governments may not be able to pursue policy on which they are elected and which they believe is in the public interest since they may be obstructed by the guardians of the interests of the Crown. According to Ian Bancroft, a former permanent secretary of the Civil Service Department, 'the Service belongs neither to politicians nor to officials but to the Crown and to the nation'. The Crown becomes a device with which civil servants can defend the 'nation' from what Ferdinand Mount, a former policy adviser to Mrs Thatcher, calls 'the instantaneous, immediate, hot-and-strong breath of public opinion . . . The civil service is a self-regulating, self-selecting, self-perpetuating, self-disciplining corps which regards loyalty to the Crown in its capacity as the embodiment of the nation as a great deal more than a mere shibboleth.'

The civil service – and experts in general – can at best only reflect *their own perception* of the public good and at worst a prejudicial view of people as unable to decide what is in their own interest. Such perceptions will almost always favour continuity against reform, since the bureaucrat will be part of a hierarchy, and his or her activity will be weighted with one eye on promotion, and so will favour the known preferences of superiors. In this way new ideas, challenging ideas and the ideas of the elected government can be filtered out by the power of the dominant institutional ethos.

In addition, membership of the European Community has greatly increased the dependence of ministers upon civil service expertise. Senior civil servants from all European Community countries meet in a body called the Committee of Permanent Representatives or COREPER. Most decisions reached in the Council of Ministers will have been agreed in advance by COREPER. These pre-negotiations between civil servants are of substantial importance, and can be used by Community civil servants to press a common agenda on the various governments. Civil servants are in a key position where they are trading information on their government's bargaining position and intentions. In negotiation they will aim to reach agreement on an agenda of 'feasible' policy options. Government objectives filter down from cabinet and ministers but the decisions are taken in a whole

network of Community committees, panels and organisations.

This may be the case with any large bureaucratic structure, but the European Community remains a special case
because of the policy-making role it gives to seventeen
appointed Commissioners. Substantial areas of government
are under the control of the Commission, which is charged
with both the initiation and execution of Community
policy. The Council of Ministers in the European Community is a law-making body and the Commission serves as its
'government'. The structure is far from democratic. And
yet more and more power is being poured into the Community. Member governments will have to concede to majority
voting in the Community on a range of issues and if they fail
to do so, the Community can use British *courts* to overturn
the policies of British governments.

Loyal but not an Opposition

The most significant of the democratic constraints on Prime
Ministerial power is the timing of a general election. But
when a large amount of power is vested in one person, and a
vote has to be cast across a multiplicity of issues determined
over the previous Parliament, the outcome cannot be a
continuous democratic accountability for government. In
addition, at just the time when the Prime Minister is most
vulnerable, party loyalty will be at its strongest.

The opposition is assumed to be the most significant of
the controls on government. An effective opposition can
embarrass the government and cause it to spend time
answering questions away from its chosen agenda, but the
effect is limited in important respects, not the least of which
is that in recent times, the opposition parties have come to
share many of the policies of the party in power. That the

opposition party represents a Prime Minister and government-in-waiting poses a permanent threat to the security of the present incumbents. But for an opposition's attacks to have any force, its alternative programme must have support and in fact the opposition's desire to be seen as a government-in-waiting can hinder its function as critic of government policy and principle.

The outcome is not effective opposition, but effective consensus – a situation not unlike that existing between the Whigs and the Tories 140 years ago.

All parties now agree on membership of the EC, on the role of NATO, on the maintenance of nuclear weapons, on the primacy of free markets and on the continuance of the war in Ireland. Her Majesty's loyal opposition seems almost to have become persuaded that its loyalty supersedes its opposition.

Government by consensus has been helped by the extension of the Select Committee system under reforms implemented in 1979. It was intended that these would give back-benchers an opportunity to prise information from civil servants and ministers. In reality party whips have come to control the appointment of individual MPs to committees and their membership reflects the balance of the parties within the House. The Select Committees have become effectively a network of coalitions, knitting government and opposition back-benchers together through a common desire to reach unanimous conclusions. They are able to extract information from civil servants and ministers on the minutiae of policy, but may not explore alternatives to policies which the government undertakes. The Permanent Secretaries, having initially viewed the committees with some trepidation, have realised that they provide an additional route by which controlled information can be officially disseminated.

This consensus is strengthened by the magic circle of the Privy Council, whose members are supposed to consult together confidentially, without risk of information 'leaking' outside. In the Parliamentary context this is an important system which maintains close relations between the government of the day and the opposition leaders. Backbenchers as a whole are excluded from the deliberations.

This club lubricates 'the usual channels' – which are the inter-party talks that go on all the time between the main front benches about the conduct of business in the House – and in a war situation, such as the Falklands in 1982, provides an opportunity for highly confidential briefings to be undertaken to win the opposition over to the acceptance of the government line. There is in this system an element of the conspiracy by the governing class against the governed which has serious implications for freedom of information and makes for an unhealthy consensus on some issues. In this sense the Privy Council is an undemocratic feudal club.

This process is reinforced by attempts to coopt those who propose radical change to the system of consensus government.

And radical politicians are vulnerable to being coopted – it is very flattering for a shadow minister to be called in and told in confidential Privy Council terms about, say, Northern Ireland affairs. Even in the Labour Party the accountability of the Parliamentary party to the national party has been to some extent undermined by a parallel system of centralised power which is buttressed by patronage.

Such temptations are used in Britain to sustain a status quo which is unfavourable to the interests of the majority of the British people.

Assaults on democracy

Britain is like a motorbike with four-wheel braking. It is amazing, given the existing constitutional and cultural constraints, that we make any progress at all. There has been a flourishing renaissance of appointed public and semi-public posts under recent Conservative governments, to the real detriment of more representative bodies. Health authorities have been restructured to reduce the number of elected representatives and to replace them with appointees, budgets have been given to the Training and Enterprise Councils (TECs), consisting of appointed businessmen and women who now control substantial public funds; Urban Development Corporations have been appointed and given control of massive budgets of upwards of £200m, such as the London Docklands Development Corporation. With wide planning and development powers previously under the control of local elected councils and accountable to their electorates, the UDCs have applied criteria for which they are accountable to no-one save the minister. And having rate-capped all councils, abolished the GLC against the wishes of the electors of London, the government is now funding a committee of prominent business 'leaders' called The London Forum, charged with the responsibility of attracting investment to the capital.

Britain's problems are intimately connected with the continuance of such aristocractic and technocratic hierarchies. Some industrialists would apparently rather be made peers, put on quangos and made Governors of the BBC, before finishing on the Arts Council, than try to be successful businessmen or women. Individuals including many labour leaders, are seduced by ribbons and ermine, and bemused by ritual and privilege. All hierarchies want to preserve rather than change institutions as each person looks upwards to please the person above, rather than downwards to provide what people below need.

The House of Lords can still present a substantial obstacle to a government, particularly one which might attempt what Conservative MP John Stokes has called 'any stupid or revolutionary law if the Commons were so minded to do such a thing'. Governments must be subject to checks and balances, but these should be democratic, not imposed by appointed and hereditary élites.

Under the 1949 Parliament Act the House of Lords can delay legislation, passed by the House of Commons, for one year, unless the legislation is a Money Bill. Therefore, because there is an inbuilt Conservative majority in the Lords, a Labour government theoretically has a life of only four years, while a Conservative government, with a majority in both Houses, has a full five-year term within which to pass legislation. Although the House of Lords will usually favour a Conservative government, its natural preference for the status quo will provide a brake on radical legislation from right or left, as the Lords defeat of the War Crimes Bill in 1991 illustrated.

But neither the 1911 nor the 1949 Acts have removed a Lords veto on subordinate legislation, *i.e.* legislation made on the authority of powers delegated under statutes passed in the Commons. As the volume of government business increases, substantial legislation is made by ministers and local authorities under delegated powers without debate in Parliament. The Lords retain the right to strike down all legislation of this type, and could put a serious brake on a government whose policies they considered 'stupid and revolutionary'.

Democratic checks and balances were provided at local level in the early years of elected local government. But today local government has been reduced to little more than a tier of administration. When local government is squeezed from the centre, central government is not just restricting political opposition but restricting the system of democratic checks and balances. If the party of government objects to what local government is doing, it should campaign locally to defeat it: local councils should come under no form of control other than by the police station, in the event of corruption, and the polling station in the event of unpopularity.

But Conservative governments of the 1980s crushed the challenge that local government posed to their power by constraining and, in the case of the GLC and the other metropolitan boroughs, eliminating local councils. Those councils that remain are forced to operate within severe financial restrictions set by government.

By law now, if local councillors vote for policies for which they have been elected which exceed centrally imposed spending limits, they can be made personally liable for any overspending judged to have taken place. Councillors may be made bankrupt or disqualified from office. No such punishment was imposed on Government ministers after the financial debacle of Black Wednesday when £10 billion of public funds were lost. Nor was there provision to hold ministers or their appointees personally to account for the millions spent on developing Canary Wharf in the Docklands fiasco.

Local government has been reduced so that unwilling councils now have a role similar to that performed by the magistrates and the Lord Lieutenants in the early nineteenth century, offering very little challenge to the power of the executive.

Official secrecy

Nowhere has lack of accountability to the democratic process been more apparent than in our security services, trusted with substantial powers which leave them free from any effective democratic control. The extraordinary complacency with which the allegations in *Spycatcher* were received was the end result of monotonous propaganda over the years that such incidents were in the interests of the Crown and the defence of national security.

A major part of the work of the security services, traditionally closely connected with the military, has been for domestic purposes. The army has intermittently put down colonial and domestic revolts, as in Northern Ireland, and the security services have been used in the surveillance of domestic activity including that of trade unionists, members of CND and workers of the National Council of Civil Liberties. That there is a role for the security services is itself an issue for the people to decide, but such a service should certainly be democratically accountable for its actions. Parliament does not have to be told what the security services are planning to do in advance, only that people should know, after the event, on what grounds phones have been tapped, on whose authority individuals have been placed under surveillance or had their homes searched, which foreign governments have been under-mined, which supported and why.

But instead, ex-members of the security services have explicitly rejected democratic control.

On a Channel 4 programme, *After Dark*, Lord Dacre, himself an ex-employee of MI6, and former Master of Peterhouse College, Cambridge, was asked whether the secret service should be democratically accountable. He replied:

> I would like to see it accountable indirectly by having the ultimate authority outside party politics, and if there were a body which consisted of respectable people, respected by all sides, then it wouldn't be dependent on the government of the day . . . It wouldn't be subject to a particular party which happened to be in power and it would be subject to the state, not to the government.

Currently the security services are free to choose their own enemy under loose definitions given at different times. In the 1970s the Labour Home Office Minister, John Harris, defined subversives as 'those who try to undermine the government of the state by violent or other means'. If you argue for constitutional reform you may be a subversive. Earlier, the Home Secretary, Maxwell Fyfe, gave a directive that the security services were free to act at a distance from ministerial control. Individual ministers, even senior members of government, have little access to security material even when it is of direct concern to them. Gerald Gardiner, Labour Lord Chancellor in 1964, one of the most senior Privy Councillors, asked to see his own security file and was denied access. The security services do remain formally accountable to the Prime Minister, but as Peter Wright demonstrated, members will flout that accountability if it conflicts with their own perception of the interests of the nation or state.

There is a complex intertwining of British and American security interests. American influence over British security was accepted during the 1950s and 60s under the royal prerogative of treaty-making as part of a deal to share American nuclear secrets and maintain a British nuclear force, notionally independent, but under American control. It was because of this link that, according to some considerable evidence, James Angleton of the CIA was able to instruct MI5 agents to place Harold Wilson, when Prime Minister, under surveillance as a suspected Soviet agent. 'The accusation was totally incredible but given the fact that Angleton was head of the CIA's Counterintelligence Division we had no choice but to take it seriously,' Wright wrote.

Wilson was not the only target of these activities, which extended to Edward Heath, who was apparently considered by some in the security services to be too weak to be trusted with the premiership. All these activities conducted against politicians and others were undertaken by a small group or groups who nonetheless had convinced themselves that their duty was to the Crown. Empowered to act by the royal prerogatives, they were also excluded from accountability by a duty of lifelong confidentiality owed to the Crown.

The whole *Spycatcher* affair, whatever the culpability of the individuals concerned, highlights a constitutional process, a structure of government, which permits state powers to be exercised against elected government and in secret.

Secrecy provides probably the most significant constraint upon effective opposition and accountable government. The new Official Secrets Act, introduced in 1988, eased some controls and allowed the disclosure of mundane matters, but extended other controls over information necessary for proper accountability. In particular the Act extended official secrecy to cover all matters concerning international affairs. The increasing integration of British policy into a European Community framework means that more and more aspects of government policy can be protected by official secrecy, if the Prime Minister so chooses.

The Prime Minister's control of information, in particular that related to the national interest, has led to Parliament being deliberately misled on several occasions. The invasion of Egypt in 1956, for example, was claimed to be in response to an Israeli attack. In reality, it was part of a pact between the Israelis, the French and the British to invade Egypt and topple Nasser. Indeed Peter Wright seems to confirm what others have claimed that 'at the beginning of the Suez crisis, MI6 developed a plan, through the London Station, to assassinate Nasser using nerve gas.'

It was also on the grounds of national security that the

prerogative was used to establish the 130 permanent American bases in Britain after the Second World War. Parliament was told that these were for training missions, although it soon became clear that they were fully operational military bases. Similar Crown powers were used to commit substantial public funds to the development of nuclear weapons in the 1940s and, more recently, to the Chevaline and Zircon projects without the knowledge or approval of Parliament.

Whereas Britain has a 30-year rule covering the release of secret information, the vast majority of US government activity is open to public scrutiny. The case of Oliver North and Peter Wright provide a very interesting comparison: Colonel North was brought before Congress for his part in the illegal selling of arms to fund right-wing political activities in Nicaragua. Peter Wright, by contrast, confessed that he took part in the destabilisation of an elected government and yet, rather than trying to establish the truth or falsity of his allegations, the government tried to silence him.

The British state is a leaky ship. Civil servants who have access to sensitive material are in a position to make damaging disclosures to the opposition front bench and can cause substantial embarrassment to the government. The Prime Minister can of course leak anything he or she pleases through lobby briefings of the press, but at the same time can initiate a leak enquiry into any disclosure of information which has not been approved by him or her (such as occurred in the Clive Ponting case, not because he was passing sensitive information to the enemy, but because he had leaked information to the British people which discredited the government). In fact the new Official Secrets Act has been reformed to plug the gaps by which civil servants could justify leaks as being in the public interest. It has also brought much tighter restrictions to bear upon ex-members of the security services to prevent repetitions of the *Spycatcher* affair.

There is some role for official secrecy, but not to keep the activity of government and the process of decision making under wraps, or to limit the ability of Parliament to enforce effective accountability. Unless the Commons can claim, on behalf of the electorate, a greater knowledge of what is happening, its role will slowly shrink back to that of ex-post-facto and ineffective auditor of decisions already taken, leaving government MPs as lobby fodder, merely rubber-stamping government decisions.

The European Community and parliamentary government

A development of potentially extraordinary significance has breathed new life into the authority of the royal prerogatives, adding greatly to their strength and to the government's freedom to implement them against the wishes of Parliament. This change came with British membership of the European Community. Membership of the Community has increased the power of *Government* and reduced the law making role of *Parliament*, transferring law-making to the executive in a manner which uses the prerogatives on a scale not seen since 1649.

Until 1972 the prerogatives could only be used with binding legal force by the Prime Minister or executive in areas that were consistent with law made in Parliament. The House of Commons could set the boundaries within which Crown powers had their freedom. Britain's entry to the European Community removed control of laws, made under the Crown prerogatives in the EC, from direct control by Parliament.

The European Community is sustained by treaties, and therefore legislation made in the Community has effect in

United Kingdom law under the prerogative. The 1972 Act, which is an enabling Act, allows Community law to become binding in United Kingdom courts without any requirement for further parliamentary approval.

Section 2(1) of the Act states that:

> All such rights, powers, liabilities, obligations and restrictions from time to time created or arising by or under the Treaties, and all such remedies and procedures from time to time provided for by or under the Treaties, as in accordance with the Treaties *are without further enactment to be given legal effect* or used in the United Kingdom shall be recognised and available in law, and be enforced, allowed and followed accordingly.

This means that law is able to be made using Crown powers which then have immediate and direct effect in British courts.

As a result there are now two law-making authorities in operation in Britain. Under the present treaty arrangements Community legislation will override any law passed in the House of Commons.

A ruling of the European Court of Justice in 1978 made this point clearly. It instructed any national court to give primacy to the provisions of Community law:

> If necessary *refusing of its own motion to apply any conflicting provision of national legislation, even if adopted subsequently* . . . it [would not be] necessary for the [national] court to request or even await the prior setting aside of such provisions by legislative or other constitutional means.

In consequence, legislation passed in the House of Commons will only become law if it does not conflict with legislation made in Brussels. Even so it will only remain law as long as the Community does not legislate to supersede it. The constitutional irony of this position is that whereas, before entry to the European Community, Crown powers could only be exercised in the legislative space left by Parliament, the position has to some degree been reversed: Parliament now only has law making power in the space left for it by Crown prerogatives exercised by British ministers in Brussels. The Crown now sets the boundaries within which the House of Commons has legislative freedom.

The legal implications of this position were demonstrated on 10 March, 1989, when the British High Court granted an interim injunction suspending the 1988 Merchant Shipping Act. The Act was referred to the European Court which overturned it on 26 July, 1991, on the grounds that it was in breach of Community law. In his judgement in the High Court Lord Justice Neill made the point clearly: 'One cannot over-emphasise that, where applicable, Community law is part of the law of England.'

Taken together, the Treaties have acquired a quasi-constitutional status in British law, giving courts the power to decide which policies are legitimate on criteria determined under the Crown prerogatives.

British governments are therefore bound by a large volume of legislation in the form of regulations *and directives* made in Brussels. This has placed very real legal obstructions in the way of any British government's free choice of policy and the right of the electors.

Entrenched in the Treaty of Rome and the Single European Act is a commitment to the free movement of labour and capital. Any policy that would seek to intervene significantly in the operation of free markets in Britain is formally against the treaty commitments and could be

66

enforced as such by the British courts.

The Treaty of Rome explicitly prohibits any support to industry which might distort competition between member states, and the Maastricht treaty, if ratified, would attempt to impose a strict budgetary discipline upon member states, forcing the Public Sector Borrowing Requirement to fall and establishing an independent European Central Bank, so effectively removing constitutional control of monetary policy from the governments of member states.

Every British government is obliged to inform the European Commission if it plans to give financial support to industry, and if the Commission decides that the aid is against Community rules, it will outlaw it. The 1974 Labour Government was forced to give way on several policies, including regional employment premiums, temporary employment subsidies and government aids to offshore drilling supplies, which were judged contrary to the laws of the Common Market. At the time of writing, the German Government is coming under pressure from the EC to limit industrial support to former East Germany which has been devastated by market forces.

Therefore if short-term market interests dictate that a factory has to close – even in circumstances where it was decided by the government that it would be in the long-term interest of the country to keep it open – the obligations imposed by the treaty might outlaw any government assistance, even if it had been a major policy in that government's manifesto to provide such assistance.

This severely limits the freedom of government and the electors to decide on policies of their own choosing. A similar situation would never be accepted in America: California cannot ban imports of goods from New Mexico or Texas, but it is quite free to subsidise its own industry.

Under the American constitution a socialist government would at least be constitutionally legal and could be elected with the freedom to carry out interventionist policies. But a government with a similar programme in Britain would be ruled to be in breach of our European treaty commitments. The Treaty of Rome has effectively put us in hand-cuffs, binding us to a constitution drawn up under Crown powers, which, to a significant degree, entrenches free-market capitalism.

Much of the European Community debate has become, quite wrongly, entangled with the idea of sovereignty. Various commentators and critics of Europe lament the inability of Parliament to have sovereign control of its own territory. But no government – or monarch for that matter – has ever enjoyed complete independence or freedom from external circumstance. As is often said, it is peculiar to speak of a reduction in the sovereignty of the British Parliament by closer membership of Europe when, in or out, Britain's economic policy is influenced by interest rates in the Bundesbank and foreign policy by resolutions in the UN and decisions within NATO. Absolute sovereignty, in this sense – especially of Parliament which is a false notion anyway – has never been possessed by anyone. There have always been important external constraints on the freedom of governments to act. It has never been true that government could do what it liked.

But it is a severe limitation of democratic government and the electors when they are to lose control of their own legal order or the laws placed on the statute book and government is not able to choose *how to respond* to external pressures or events.

Even were the government fully accountable to the British people, the people are clearly not in a position to control the basic rules governing society and their lives if laws made in Brussels can over-rule domestic law made in Parliament.

In short, membership of the European Community has had the effect of establishing a superior and unelected legal power with binding force in British courts. The European Court declared in 1964 that:

> Unlike ordinary international treaties, the EEC treaty established its own legal order, which is incorporated into legal systems of the Member States and to which the courts of the Member States are bound . . . The states relinquished, albeit in limited areas, their sovereign rights and thus created a body of law applicable to the nationals and to themselves.

The British Parliament has no power to overturn individually any laws made in Brussels, but can only repeal them *en masse* by withdrawal from the Treaty of Rome. This constitutes a degree of entrenchment which gives *all* European Community legislation, and not only the Treaties, the effective power of constitutional law – allowing courts to strike down British legislation. What would happen to a government unwilling to recognise a particular item of European legislation, but equally unwilling to withdraw from the Treaties? The legal position would be clear, and national courts, while the member state remained signatory to the Treaties, would have to uphold the supremacy of European legislation even though the government of the member state might have counteracted it with national statute.

European Community legislation imposes specific limits on legislative freedom. Membership of the Community has not merely altered constitutional arrangements once and for all, but also allows a continuous re-writing of the rules within which Parliament may be left to operate. Clearly, while the Community remains undemocratically structured, this constitutes a breach of the principle that people should be able to determine the rules and principles which govern their lives.

But whilst membership of the European Community has undoubtedly narrowed the sphere of freedom open to Parliament, it has greatly increased the powers available to ministers.

The Council of Ministers of the European Community is the legislature, passing or defeating proposals which come from the Commission. Here government ministers meet in secret to debate and vote upon Community policy which may later become law. The European Council, comprising the heads of state of the Community members, sets the broad policy agenda and increasingly takes a leading role in settling major policy issues. These bodies have effective control over Community law making. The potential political importance of this for the power of the British executive should be clear.

In particular Parliament increasingly has to abdicate its law-making or legislative function to government ministers who are given a substantial degree of freedom in Community negotiations. Ministers do not allow the House of Commons to mandate them in advance of Community decisions and when decisions have been made, Parliament has no power to repeal them. This creates an opportunity for a law which is unlikely to be slipped through the House of Commons by any government with a slim majority, but which is acceptable to the European Community members, to be brought into legal effect in Britain by passing it through the Council of Ministers. After this, if it is ratified by the remaining Community procedures, it will acquire a quasi-constitutional status in British law and Parliament may be unable to repeal it without a full withdrawal from the Treaties of the Community.

While the strength of government has been increased

with respect to Parliament, the strength of the British government, with respect to the Community itself, has been altered by the increasing use of majority voting in the Council of Ministers. The use of majority voting can allow the Community to impose legislation in British courts against the wishes of the government. Since 1966 the Luxembourg compromise, established as a convention to appease De Gaulle, has provided protection allowing governments a right of veto on legislation 'where very important interests are at stake'. But this protection has come under attack. The increasing use of majority voting under the 1986 Single European Act, whose provisions were agreed by all the member states, makes it difficult if not impossible for any national government to claim a vital interest veto. The Commons foreign affairs committee declared itself to be: 'extremely sceptical about the ability of British governments to invoke the Luxembourg compromise in future, particularly in those areas of decision making which are now to be made subject to majority voting with the support and encouragement of HM Government'.

If governments are unable to veto legislation they don't like, then scrutiny of European Community legislation in Commons committees, intended to attempt to make government activity in Brussels come under a degree of Parliamentary examination, will be frustrated. The committees are in any case relatively ineffective in the scrutiny of Community law: they rely heavily on the government and the civil service for information and are increasingly overwhelmed by the flood of legislation from Brussels. But clearly, even if they desired to affect an amendment to Community legislation, and were able to secure the agreement of a minister to do so, the effectiveness of Parliamentary committees to secure amendments on subjects which can be decided by a qualified majority vote would not be effective.

This diminishes the strength of Parliament still further. But peculiarly it has added to the strength of government ministers. The decreasing use of the national veto makes negotiation between ministers of member states in advance of discussion in Brussels absolutely critical. The enhanced role given to British ministers and to the Prime Minister adds considerably to their personal influence in Community policy making.

Against the striking impact which membership of the European Community has on the British system of government, it is argued in Europe's favour that is can provide Britain with far more progressive legislation and rights than will come from domestic government. Cynicism with British government encourages people to look to Brussels to save them from the mess. Many people have lost faith in the British political system to recognise their claims. The Community is pressing for the social chapter to protect working conditions. But this is yet another expression of the British tendency to look to people at the top to solve problems. While the Government was able to negotiate an 'opt out' from legislation to limit the working week, claiming this to be a victory for workers' rights, and has been able to exclude itself from the social chapter and to campaign for Britain's right to be a low wage economy, it has also used Community law to entrench market forces which allow companies to close factories and remove their investments from Britain without any check by British law.

People should be asking why Britain cannot have a social chapter of its own, why we don't have progressive legislation to protect the environment, why the Government has so drastically reduced the power of local democracy, why Scotland and Wales and the regions of England continue to be run like colonies from London. The answer to these questions is not to be found in Brussels, and the cost of trying to find it there is immense, in terms of our capacity for democratic self-government.

Conclusion

British democracy is fragile and under great threat. The monarch retains, in law, substantial powers, such that a coup under the Crown would be quite legal.

The Prime Minister has ultimate control of the main royal prerogatives and with the loyalty ensured by patronage and party discipline, he or she is able to exercise them beyond the democratic control of the House of Commons.

Membership of the European Community has breathed new life into the royal prerogatives, weakening the House of Commons and the electorate, and introducing constraints in law upon the freedom of British people to use Parliament to achieve their specific goals.

The position described by Bagehot in 1867 in *The English Constitution* has effectively been reversed. Bagehot described the Monarch as the 'dignified' element of the constitution, providing legitimacy to the disguised 'efficient' exercise of power by Parliament. Today it would be more accurate to describe the House of Commons as the dignified part of the constitution, which is there to 'excite and preserve the reverence of the population' while the powers of the Crown, controlled by the Prime Minister, are the efficient part 'by which [government], in fact, works and rules'.

But the crux of the matter is not that the Prime Minister has unlimited power – the Prime Minister is quite clearly not a dictator – but that the structures which determine what is politically feasible are generally undemocratic. The Prime Minister is able to use the prerogatives, and in particular the powers of patronage, to create a distance between his or her own executive actions and the controlling influence of the cabinet, and in particular the control of the House of Commons, where the party and MPs, particularly in the case of the Labour Party, can quite properly constrain the Prime Minister's freedom of action. Once isolated from the source of democratic authority the Prime Minister will be open to extra-Parliamentary action from powerful interest groups and élites, not the least of which are the City, big business, the European Community, the civil service, the military, the media, and, in the case of a Labour government, the unions, not to mention international pressures from foreign agencies and governments.

The Prime Minister will make compromises in order to retain the support of these groups and remain in power. As a result the semi-elected Parliament is reduced to one of a number of centres of influence which collectively determine the exercise of the prerogatives.

IV

Rights under Capitalism

The enjoyment of property and the direction of industry are considered, in short, to require no social justification, because they are regarded as rights which stand by their own virtue, not functions to be judged by the success by which they contribute to a social purpose. Today, that doctrine.. is still the practical foundation of social organisation.

R. H. Tawney, 1921

A constitution is only a means to an end; it is a mechanism to advance people's interests and goals collectively, in determining the kind of society they want. The establishment by and large wants government which manages a capitalist free-market economy in a hands-off fashion and minimum constitutional guarantees; the majority of people want a society which provides decent housing for all citizens, a right to work for a living wage and fair conditions, and a right to a good standard of living for retired people. Whatever, by voting, people decide they want, it becomes the business of government to do its best to implement these choices. Citizenship, under the

Commonwealth of Britain Bill, means the ability to choose and control the conditions of society.

Central to this control is the statement of basic principles set out in the Charter of Rights.

There are currently popular arguments in favour of limiting rights to a pre-set list. Rights which are said to support democracy – so-called procedural rights – are separate, it is argued, from claims to economic or social rights such as a minimum income, health provision, legal aid or decent housing. Those who now enjoy power contend that only procedural rights should form part of a constitution because these rights are said to be politically *neutral*, providing the necessary conditions for democracy, whereas the inclusion of social and economic rights would embed a radical political view into the constitution which will limit the power of the powerful. This is why they prefer such matters to be decided by the government of the day, so that contentious economic and social matters decided by ordinary legislation can also be repealed by Parliament.

This position is being advanced by many powerful groups in Britain in order to limit any future Bill of Rights to a specific minimal set of protections for the citizen, protections which are no longer in line with the diverse range of cultural and political opinion in late 20th century Britain.

In an editorial comment on Labour's proposals for a Charter of Rights made at the 1991 conference, the *Independent* argued that 'Economic matters are not appropriate for constitutional charters'. This disguised the *Independent*'s dislike of many of the ideas discussed. Disapproval at the inclusion of rights to equal treatment for gay men and women led the editorial to ask 'Would a Labour government lower the age of consent for male homosexuals and legitimise homosexual "marriage"?'

The statement that claims must be politically neutral is another way of saying that the rights deemed neutral enjoy general support; but they are not free from moral or political value or above debate. No rights can be. All rights are ultimately political and all constitutions are political. The campaigns for the right to vote were highly charged politically. Rights to the ownership of private property are extraordinarily political with consequences which constrain society to a particular set of outcomes. Free association, free speech, and *habeas corpus* have had and continue to have immensely important political implications. They also continue to enjoy broad support. Limited procedural rights serve to outline a set of particular objectives to which people are alleged to give consent as the governing principles of society, *i.e.* they protect a rather weak liberal capitalist democracy.

A more pragmatic objection to economic and social rights in the constitution is that governments may not be able to protect or deliver them. If they fail to do so, it is argued, a constitution will lose legitimacy, threatening the democratic system it protects. Constitutions which promise much and are unable to deliver may lose popular support.

But the aim should not be to try to construct a written constitution which will endure for ever, rather to assert and protect certain basic values and at the same time to develop a culture which enables the system of recognised rights to be advanced or altered when dominant values change.

Another argument is that social and economic rights involve governments in spending money whereas procedural rights do not. But elections do not come free and neither do the substantial legal and police services which protect property.

The real reason why economic and social rights are excluded is firstly because influential groups would stand to lose considerably if they were recognised and secondly because many who favour limited constitutional reform see the support of 'the great and the good' as necessary to its success. Charter 88, according to one of its council mem-

77

bers Paul Hirst, 'draws on political activists in all three opposition parties, eminent judges and lawyers, leading figures in the arts, prominent academics and leading writers', and this may be why Charter 88 does not campaign for social and economic rights which might cause friction in its political alliance.

Arguments against social and economic rights usually reflect prejudice or opportunist pragmatism. Rights do not have to be universal or indivisible or cost-free, they simply have to be agreed upon.

The importance of including social and economic rights in any proposal for constitutional reform is to establish once and for all that the nature of the economic system should be a matter for public choice, and that free-market capitalism should not be accepted without any discussion of the rich variety of alternatives.

To assert that people should choose and control their economic system sounds radical after fifteen years of governments pronouncing that no alternative is possible. Unlike civil laws, economic laws are imposed on people with all the authority of immutable laws of nature. But the economy is created by people, supported by government intervention, regulation, statute and subsidy, and implemented in such a way that it gives substantial wealth and power to a privileged few, while the majority face a life of relentless work, stress and periodic financial insecurity.

The concentration of wealth gives individuals considerable political power. Money can be used to gain influence, particularly when the powers of state are only loosely controlled by elected bodies and so heavily concentrated in Westminster. The unequal distribution of wealth, income and status which the laws of capitalism promote, not only gives the rich greater political power than the poor, and greater resouces with which to pursue their own interests, but it elevates people to positions of influence on the basis of their gender and their race.

Political power should, wherever possible, be brought under democratic control, so that the people affected by the adoption and operation of a particular economy should be able to hold to account those to whom that power is *given*.

After all, a government which supposedly represents the interests of all the people subsidises and supports the current form of the economy, and it is the ingenuity and effort of all those who work which allows the country to produce wealth. Those same people are assured that the economy is a natural fact – a necessity – and the inequalities and insecurities it generates are not subject to choice, but to chance.

People would do well to ask themselves how many of their ambitions and aspirations derive from the type of economic system they inhabit and the insecurity and exhaustion it creates, and question the sense and purpose of a society where control of a large portion of life is abdicated under contract in the labour market, and where immense creativity and potential is stifled by the need to do difficult and repetitive tasks in order to earn a wage.

But the economic system persists because they suffer it. It may be the case that if people were to be given a choice they would choose to preserve what they have. But they should at least examine alternatives. Not least because the economy itself is very different from the orthodox image of free-markets and equal exchange which people are encouraged to see, and from the mirage that much of the inequality that exists simply reflects a reward for hard work.

The worship of markets

In spite of the parliamentary consensus which has grown up in support of market forces in recent years, free-market capitalism is manifestly failing here and in Western Europe, while the myth that there is no other real choice continues to be peddled. There is no bucking the market, we are told, and no alternative to the devastating economic turbulence into which the economy was thrown in 1979 and to which it is still victim. People have been persuaded that there is nothing they can do about it.

In reality, market forces are often ignored within the capitalist economy, which is not characterised by hundreds of thousands of small competing businesses, but by large corporations, banks and financial institutions which exercise immense power over market outcomes using their own corporate 'civil service' bureaucracies. These bureaucracies plan the development of new markets and new products, they plan the allocation of labour and resources within the company to achieve production targets, and they plan hostile takeovers and resist takeover bids by competitors with no regard for constitutional rights of citizens.

Nor will firms always conduct their business through the market. Often markets will be shared by firms who choose to collude rather than to compete. Some of the deals undertaken by firms outside the market have caused regulators to say enough is enough. But in several instances, information about such activities in the Eighties was kept secret from workforces who depended on the survival of the firms for their livelihood. Events unveiled in the 1980s by the Blue Arrow, Guinness, Maxwell and BCCI cases would have been paraded as the inevitable corruption of communism in any Eastern bloc country. In Britain they are viewed as exceptional, the consequence of slight oversights by regulating authorities combined with individual vice. The free market that is worshipped in the west has been anything but free in some sectors, while the 'liberation' of market forces heralded by the governments of the Eighties has ushered in a period of low growth, low investment and high unemployment, in contrast to the rapid re-employment of servicemen and women and reconstruction of industry which took place under a highly planned economy at the end of World War Two. There has been no history of completely free markets in British economic management, and at periods when areas of the economy were kept under greater control, the economy as a whole actually performed a great deal better.

The present British economic system is treated as if it were an objective immutable fact of life, and unemployment something that has to be tolerated. But the economic system, like the political system, has been fashioned by institutional developments throughout history. Trade dates back to the days of barter, but the end of the system of common land, and the enclosure acts, began a process of private ownership of the means of livelihood which left many with no other way to earn a living than to sell their property, i.e. their labour. The 'free market' since then emerged out of competition, ownership, and trade union activity through a political process which initially only recognised property or land as a qualification.

Capitalism has survived because it is powerful, not because it offers people the best or most worthwhile lifestyle or supports the rights of consumers, citizens or workers. In many countries market forces inflict immense hardship. Low prices for harvests whose markets are flooded by western surpluses help keep African countries in famine, and when grain prices are favourable, the money earned is either used to repay loans to western banks or to buy arms from western firms, to continue civil wars, many of which are the product of national boundaries and Cold War politics inflicted on ex-colonial peoples. The New World Order that is needed is one which could prevent half

81

the world starving while the other half has food to burn, can have economies which succeed without having to export arms, and which recognises the rights of other cultures to organise their own economic systems.

Many of the problems facing the British, if not the world economy, stem from market forces having too much influence and there being too little intervention and planning in defence of human values protected by the state. No-one calls for market forces to regulate everything. The armed forces and the judiciary will always be maintained by the state. Indeed markets cannot survive without a system of law enforcement to protect rights to private property. Without some institution to enforce contracts and private property, the capitalist market system would crumble, and without regulation to control the activities of large firms and protect consumers and workers, the outcomes would be unacceptable. But for many so called new liberals the sole function of the state should be a minimal one. Groups like the Institute for Economic Affairs and individuals like Professor Hayek, Milton Friedman, and many 'Thatcherite' conservatives favour the 'rolling back of the state' to expose everything to market power. The Oxford fellow John Gray makes the point clearly: 'No system of government', he says, 'in which property rights and basic liberties are open to revision by temporary political majorities can be regarded as satisfying liberal requirements. For this reason, an authoritarian type of government may sometimes do better from a liberal standpoint than a democratic regime': classic repudiation of human rights and their role in shaping democracy.

The political right has in tandem with the liberation of market forces been justifying economic policy in which government has no responsibility for economic effects, and establishing a new consensus behind market forces and capitalism. What matters in this new consensus is the level

82

of income tax, the size of state spending, and the smooth operation of the market untrammelled by financial deficits. Economic objectives are now determined by the needs of capitalist markets. Policy is to be geared to profit maximisation and economic growth, and this is achieved by letting market forces reduce wage levels without interference from trade unions. The rendering of market forces as non-political has been endorsed by the European Single Market, and through moves towards closer European Monetary Union, and has been the basis of calls for the Bank of England to be made independent of government control, either in its own right, or as part of a European network of independent national banks.

The removal of regulatory mechanisms has led to an absurd level of uncertainty and pessimism in the economy contributed by the people to a sense of neglect of their interests. Not so many years ago, high unemployment was what was meant by a recession. Now a recession has become something for economists to declare to have begun or ended, regardless of unemployment. For most people the recession will not be over when the City regains confidence and the FT index climbs 100 points. Recession means business closure, job losses and low incomes.

The judgements of financiers and city bankers on economic issues are being adopted as an established orthodoxy rather than as reflecting a particular interest, to the exclusion usually of small businesses or trade unions. This bias is a mirror image of government economic policy of the kind which has left the economy vulnerable to speculative gambling; £10 billion pounds of treasury funds were lost on 'Black Wednesday', September 1992, when the pound was unceremoniously expelled from the ERM.

The result of the unleashing of market forces and

credit was the consumer boom, rising inflation, four years of interest rates over 10 per cent, and disastrous increase in imports and a recession which has destroyed jobs, put many people in hock to their banks, created tremendous insecurity and led to over three million people unable to earn a living. Utilities were sold short, giving share-holders quick returns. Collectively these policies fuelled a boom in financial markets while manufacturing was struggling to recover the level of output it had achieved in 1979. The financial speculation finally fell over its own feet in the October 1987 stock market crash. It is precisely the flexibility and volatility of markets – in particular of financial markets – which make them poor environments in which to create the certainty needed by producers and which eliminate the hopes which a Charter of Rights seeks to revive.

Yet, despite this abject failure, there is still the refrain that there is no alternative. Planning and industrial intervention are anathema. Businesses are trusted to instigate strategies in the public interest but local authorities are assumed incapable even of policies to create jobs and rebuild local communities. Government policy in the 1980s was specifically designed to distance local government from intervening in industrial regeneration. The Urban Development Corporations set up to rebuild areas like the East End docks, and the Government's Enterprise Zones, created areas of the country attractive to business because of substantial tax breaks, and because almost all local planning restrictions were removed. Docklands in London was heavily financed and freed from planning restrictions to attract foreign banks to London at an eventual projected cost of £5 billion. The outcome in Docklands was to create a vast office complex served by no transport links, which no-one wanted to work in, and which the government feels compelled to bail out. The GLC by contrast ran extremely popular economic policies, from local cooperatives regenerating neighbourhoods to the *Fares Fair* policy which cut public transport costs. The reaction of the Conservatives was to use the courts to ban the scheme, on the grounds that the GLC had a 'fiduciary responsibility' to the ratepayers, deemed more important than its democratic responsibility to its electors.

These more recent examples of the dismantling of democratic bodies in the interests of profit were part and parcel of the abandonment of the economy to free markets which left people undefended against market forces. As a result, economic inequality has got far worse. According to the low pay unit, inequalities in pay are larger now than at any time in the past century. Inequalities of wealth generally are also extreme. The poorest 50 per cent of the population in 1989 had only 6 per cent of the nation's personal wealth, a fall of 9 per cent from 1980.

The majority of people rely on selling their labour to survive. This is the unique feature of the economic system we have created. Under feudalism, a serf had to work to survive, but had access to *common* land, possessing, collectively with others, the means to a livelihood. Capitalism transforms everything but sea and air into private property and private wealth, allowing them to be owned indefinitely, and protecting them from future seizure by a powerful legal system defending private property rights. Feudal peasants had private property too, but they also had recourse to a community-owned means of livelihood separate from the vagaries of market transactions.

Capitalism, by appropriating all land and all machinery and factories as private property, removes from the vast majority the right to work outside a system of market regulation and market discipline and hence any real control over their lives. Instead people's labour is transformed into a commodity like any other, and workers are valued for their productivity, marketable attributes, flexibility, scarcity and the fact that they offer an employer value for money. But while the vast majority who are compelled to work to earn a living also have to depend on public provision for the education of their children, the health of their family and their pension when they retire, a minority derive sufficient income from investments to do without the assistance of the state. Despite all protestations that we are a society of classless consumers, bar a minority described as the underclass, the real division is still between those who subsist on their earnings, be they doctor, artist, bus driver, barrister, and those who subsist on income from someone else's labour.

The labour market works like any other respecting the laws of supply and demand with the consequence that it places different values on different backgrounds, education, skills and gender. Some skills are flexible and relatively plentiful. Many people have the skills to be a cleaner and the pay is low. Many people could learn bus driving and therefore in spite of a high demand for bus drivers in London pay is relatively low. But fewer people can qualify or pay for training as a barrister. The demand is less, but the supply is even lower. Barristers don't necessarily work harder than bus drivers – the vast difference in pay reflects the relative scarcity of barristers as a result of the imposition of artificial barriers.

In addition, a deliberate policy of high unemployment has kept pay claims low by the permanent threat of a pool of labour. The high supply of unemployed labour, artificially created and sustained by government policy, has led to the income of the poorest fifth of the population falling between 1979 and 1989 while the income of the richest fifth has risen by over a third. So much for the free market.

Restricted entry to the bar, and other occupations, begins at school. Low achievers leave school by the age of sixteen. Those with good GCSE results win access to A-level education, and the 'best' go on to university. And Oxford and Cambridge graduates, despite all assumptions in the 1960s and 1970s about the decline of elitism, have recolonised, or remained in control of, the BBC, the civil service and the judiciary, in absurdly disproportionate numbers.

Capitalism leaves people no choice but to take their chances selling their labour in this highly rigged market which tilts the balance against the powerless – the majority – and towards the powerful.

Market forces do not have power and efficiency in excess of all other economic systems. Free market capitalism is not as fixed and immutable as the sunrise. It is a changing and evolving system sustained by human institutions and human ingenuity and often not free at all. The price mechanism supposedly coordinates and determines the production of goods in capitalism but is so imperfect a way of communicating information that businesses rely upon extensive market research, product testing, and mass advertising. The resources spent by companies and governments researching the peculiarities of capitalism and trying to forecast its outcomes, are immense.

There is no inevitability about current inequalities arising out of so-called free-market capitalism just as there was no inevitability about the West African slave trade of the 17th century, although no doubt black slaves were told it was bad luck they were born black.

Decent income and wealth are as important a means to the equality of status which is citizenship as any of the other entitlements provided for in a Bill of Rights. The process needs to be continued to extend the idea of equal status into the economic relationship between employer and employee, and to the more fundamental relationship between those who own wealth and who are given freedom to act to increase it, and those without substantial wealth who are only given freedom to choose between a range of jobs and wages for which they are qualified.

Fairness should be extended to the treatment of labour and finance or capital. While companies have been given extensive freedom to move capital around the world, the free movement of labour is heavily managed by immigration controls which are biased towards those with investment capital. A factory can close with no period of notice, but workers must have a ballot before they close a company for a day.

There is no reason why flows of capital should not be managed in the same way as flows of people. Movements of capital have a major effect on the economy of a country, and provide those who control it with extensive political influence.

Rules over ownership of capital, like ownership of a car, should limit its detrimental use in society. Constraints on capital could make its use accountable to the needs of society rather than to the desire for profit.

Extending democratic accountability over capital might start with the removal of its control of the workplace. Currently, the governance of firms lies in the hands of managers who are technically responsible to majority shareholders. While the property qualification of the franchise for electing governments was finally removed at the beginning of the century, property rights still define who has control of the place of work. Industrial democracy would go some way to restoring the balance of power in the workplace. In particular it might provide one way of limiting the immense influence given to the small number of wealthy people who continue to own and control the British media by giving the power to appoint and dismiss management and editorial staff to the printers and journalists rather than to the shareholders.

The impact such a change might have highlights the extent to which economic power is *inevitably* political. It is as important that people control the choice of underlying principles for the economy as it is that they control the choice of procedural rights which support democracy. People should be free to decide for themselves how to organise their workplace, their local community and the national economy for the country as a whole. The social and economic rights established by the Commonwealth of Britain Bill would go some way towards building this broader concept of democracy and citizenship, re-establishing the control of democracy over the productive forces in a way which could allow people to have the economy work for them and for their needs, rather than for people to have to continue to spend their lives working for the needs of the economy.

V

Towards a Commonwealth of Britain and Europe

It should be borne in mind that there is nothing more difficult to handle, more doubtful of success, and more dangerous to carry through than initiating changes in a state's constitution. The innovator makes enemies of all those who prospered under the old order . . . and only lukewarm support is coming from those who would prosper under the new.

Niccolo Machiavelli, 1513

British subjects, European citizens

Britain has for centuries accepted the absurd notion that the nation is glued together by common loyalty, as subjects, to a hereditary sovereign. Successive kings and queens have enjoyed enormous theoretical and practical power, some but not all of which is now graciously exercised with the advice and consent of the Queen's Prime Minister and the 'Lords Spiritual and Temporal and the Commons in parliament assembled'.

Now, under the Maastricht Treaty of European Union,

all British subjects are to be magically transformed into citizens of this new union under the effective administrative, financial and legal control of appointed Commissioners, central bankers and judges all of whom are committed by the treaty to the principles of monetary stability and the 'free movement of capital and labour'.

These two completely contradictory constitutional arrangements have one thing in common – neither of them has been put to the people of this country for endorsement and therefore neither can be said to carry the democratic legitimacy that such an endorsement alone could provide.

In short we have always been governed, and are in the future always to be governed, under arrangements that have been imposed from above without our agreement or consent.

It may even be that the somewhat sullen acceptance of the Maastricht Treaty by the House of Commons, a treaty which the public is having forced down its throat, is possible because of the centuries of experience of that undemocratic monarchical system.

Critics of the monarchy are likely to be thought anti-British or unpatriotic, and critics of Maastricht as anti-European and nationalistic.

Both charges embody the simple assumption that the status quo both in Britain and the Community must never be questioned and that no serious alternative exists for the governments of either; and those who advocate an alternative way are misguided or stupid, if not dangerous and subversive.

Indeed, so strong are the pressures now to conform to the twin systems in London and Brussels that alternatives are rarely discussed. The two constitutional Bills advanced by this book offer specific and detailed alternatives both for the British and European arrangements. The Commonwealth of Britain Bill offers a new constitution for this country and the Commonwealth of Europe Bill suggests a looser and wider form of cooperation across the continent as a whole.

Each Bill contains the same *political, legal, social and economic rights*, and for the same reason, namely that the best and most durable foundation of any system of government must be the rights of those who are to be joined together under common laws; there is nothing more in it than that, but it is a great deal fairer and more sensible than a notion of personal allegiance to a monarch or a rigid concept of 'monetary stability on a level playing field' – as if life was a game of economic football in the Olympics.

Since nobody takes the oath of allegiance seriously or is persuaded that money supply can be a substitute for a moral code, a set of human aspirations in a constitution is a plausible proposition, and will provide a bench mark by which we can reasonably judge our performance as a society.

The Commonwealth of Britain Bill*

The Commonwealth of Britain Bill proposes a democratic, secular, federal Commonwealth comprising the nations of England, Scotland and Wales dedicated to the maintenance of the welfare of all its citizens.

This statement of a set of clear objectives for a society and their entrenchment in the Constitution marks a complete change in intention and sweeps away the mythology of monarchy and all the hierarchical structures which underpin it.

Neither the constitution nor the Charter of Rights lays

* See Appendix 1

92

down any ideological test or enshrines any political philosophy – as an Islamic or Marxist state might do or as has occurred in the Treaty of Rome. But they do say that whatever ideology may be adopted by a political party and endorsed by the electorate it must respect certain human rights.

The political rights set out include the right to freedom of speech and of assembly and association, of religious faith and the right to vote.

They also extend to the right of privacy from surveillance or interference – which would curtail the power of the security services – and to freedom of information, which would break down the secretiveness associated with much of the operation of the present government. The Charter extends rights to freedom of movement and to asylum as well as to conscientious objection to military service, an important initiative long overdue to those pacifists and others whose conscience over the use of arms has overriden their duty to obey the law.

Even in this narrow area of political rights a substantial advance has been made on the almost total absence of rights for a nation of subjects.

The legal rights begin with modest claims, reaffirming the rights of freedom from arbitrary arrest and of a hearing before a jury made up of other citizens together with the presumption of innocence until proved guilty.

But they go further, making cruel and degrading treatment, and capital punishment, illegal; providing for legal advice and services free at the point of use, on the same basis that the NHS was first envisaged, and prohibiting discrimination on the grounds of race, sex or sexual preference, colour, religious or political conviction or disability.

These latter provisions make deep inroads into the practice of the law and deliberately limit the power of the courts to disregard such factors in reaching their judgments.

Radical as the political and legal rights might be, when compared to existing practice, they are nothing to the social rights laid down in the Charter, rights that would provide everybody with entitlement to useful work, proper housing, recreation, to access to a full range of cultural activities, good health care, lifelong education, and to dignity in retirement.

The rights also set out the entitlement of women to control their own fertility, and to free and equal access to child care.

More generally all citizens should have access to a healthy environment, a media free from governmental or commercial domination and access to personal information held by any public authority.

These rights go well beyond what has ever been set down before; and will be denounced or disregarded as absurd and even dangerous in raising hopes that cannot be realised.

But the point in including them is to set out perfectly legitimate aspirations by which governments can reasonably be judged, and to provide a continual check upon policies that may have different and contradictory objectives based upon a conscious decision that popular rights can be ignored or overridden.

Moreover, a statement in the constitution spelling out the entitlement of everyone to a good life has an educational role to play in raising aspirations, and such an attempt should be made.

The final section of the Charter of Rights makes a daring challenge to the assumed supremacy of the economically powerful *vis à vis* the economically weak. It lays down that everyone is entitled to useful work for a living wage, to belong to a trade union and withdraw their labour, to representation in industry on a democratic basis, to adequate social benefits, and to freedom from taxation in excess of an ability to pay.

Clearly, the provision of these rights all the time to everybody would not be possible, but any Parliament failing in its responsibility would be subject to the scrutiny of a Commissioner of Human Rights on the extent of its shortfall. In fact such a principle has been adopted by the United Nations in the universal declaration of human rights, and though it has been honoured more in the breach than the observance, nobody dares recommend its repeal on that account.

The present Parliamentary Commissioner (or Ombudsman) investigates maladministration in government which may adversely affect individuals and sees to it that Parliament responds. A Commissioner for Human Rights would extend these powers to cover the Charter of Rights and bring abuses or refusal of rights to the attention of Parliament.

Inextricably linked with the role of the Parliamentary Commissioner for Human Rights is that of magistrates, appointed at present in secret by the Lord Chancellor (using the Crown prerogative). Given the power and importance of the magistracy in local communities, the Bill follows the precedent of the American system, that magistrates should be elected by voters in the areas under their jurisdiction from a panel of suitable candidates. This would extend the accountability of the law considerably.

In parallel with the reform of the Lord Chancellor's responsibilities is the idea of a National Legal Service. The current high cost of legal action can make a mockery of our judicial system, preventing litigants from going to court. Law centres have begun to develop in Britain and a national network of such centres could form the basis for a new structure of legal services available to all. Lawyers, like doctors, police and other professionals must accept their public service obligation.

The Charter of Rights makes the leap from the ballot box – which gives legitimacy to the political system – to the consent of the people for the *economic* system, and it must inevitably lead to a change in that system. This Charter goes far further than the draft Bills of Rights, enforceable by the courts, that constitutional reformers have been advocating in order to limit the powers of government and to protect private property.

In short, the Charter is a massive expansion of the potential for democratic power diffusing not only through Parliament but through industry and services at every level.

The principles

The provisions of the Bill itself provide the framework within which these rights might be achieved and are underpinned by certain principles:

- All political power is decentralised as far as is practicable so that decision-making takes place as close as possible to the people it affects.
- All political power is accountable, and all hereditary institutions, including the monarchy and the House of Lords, should end and be replaced by elected ones.
- There is 50 per cent statutory representation of women in public elected bodies – the House of Commons, the House of the People, local authorities and magistracies.
- The voting age is reduced to sixteen.
- The right to vote is based solely upon permanent residence.
- Oaths taken by all those in power and authority over

others shall be to uphold the constitution.
- The church and state are separate.
- Offices now held by patronage are, wherever practicable, subject to election or confirmation.
- The constitution and all amendments to it to be ratified by Referenda

Decentralisation of power

The principle of decentralisation appears in the Bill in many forms, in accordance with the needs of the localities, the regions, and the nations that comprise the present United Kingdom; England, Scotland and Wales will have their own national parliaments, exercising formidable powers in their own nations.

These national parliaments, each of which would have equal representation of women, would enjoy legislative and administrative power, subject only to the overriding interest of the Commonwealth in matters common to the three countries that would comprise it in respect of defence, foreign policy and the control of the currency.

The Bill is not a charter for separatism but for self-government within a framework which would bring Scottish, English and Welsh members to the Commonwealth Parliament to debate and legislate on matters of overall interests to the three nations.

Home rule for Scotland was one of Keir Hardie's commitments in the early days of the Labour Party and it has reappeared time and again since the Act of Union which united the two kingdoms of England and Scotland in 1707.

The principality of Wales – so called because it is still spoken of as the fiefdom of the Prince of Wales – entrenches the idea that the Welsh people owe a special allegiance to an English prince imposed upon them by

Edward I and consolidated by Henry VIII in the sixteenth century. The Bill recognises the equal claim of Wales to self-government.

But England is also entitled to its own cultural and political identity. The cultural identity of the English has been submerged by a history of dominating the United Kingdom and the world, such that the common people of England have been persuaded that in return for status as subjects of a King or Queen-Emperor, they somehow shared the glory of that Empire. In fact England, like Scotland and Wales is the colony that never secured its own liberation from that monarchical power.

Northern Ireland must be free, as it would be under the Bill, to determine its own future by the termination of British jurisdiction. It deserves detailed examination.

The war in Ireland, the origins of which go back over many centuries, was worsened by the partition imposed by Britain in 1921. In August 1969 the British Cabinet decided to send in troops to deal with an outbreak of violence in the province but the situation has continued to deteriorate. Over this period there have been 16,000 explosions, 3,000 people killed, and another 33,000 injured.

The total cost of this emergency, taking account of the military, police, legal and compensation claims at current prices has been estimated to amount to £14.5 billion.

Every policy that has been followed has failed and although there have been some talks with some leaders in the North and an Anglo-Irish agreement has been signed opening up a dialogue between the London and Dublin Governments, Sinn Fein has been excluded from any of these discussions.

There are many people, probably a majority in Britain, who believe that this is not an Irish problem but a British problem in Ireland and that the termination of British jurisdiction – in short that Britain should cease to claim its right to govern the province – is the only way of dealing with it, allowing the Irish, North and South, to find their own solutions to the problem of their relations.

Liberating local government

Decentralisation of power would revolutionise the efficacy of local government. Historically, the limitations on local authorities have always been more severe than those applying to private companies, which enjoy general powers constrained only within the framework of law; therefore decentralisation of power extending to local authorities general powers enabling them to act in any way that has not been declared specifically illegal by Parliament is a breakthrough in constitutional reform.

There is nothing in the memorandum of association of a private company that would prevent it from enlarging, changing the products it produces or taking over by purchase other companies, and possibly even becoming an international conglomerate.

Local councils by contrast have been strictly constrained by the sole duty to undertake only those functions allocated to it by central government. Under the Municipal Corporations Act of 1835 a great flowering of local government occurred and immense advantages to local communities developed once the dead hand of the magistrates had been lifted. In Birmingham for example after the election of the first council in 1838, local initiative developed over the next 70 years resulting in the steady establishment of a police force, the opening of the city asylum, the control of roads, sewers, lighting, sanitary arrangements, public buildings, markets and baths.

In 1861 came a public library, followed by an art gallery, a school board, the appointment of a medical officer of health and the opening of the municipal hospital in 1874.

The city took over the supply of gas and water, and at the beginning of this century operated the tramways. A municipal savings bank, a municipal orchestra and a municipal airport followed.

Though London was late into the field the election of the first London County Council in 1889 paved the way for equally adventurous services and democratic London government was the object of great pride.

In recent years the trend has been the absolute opposite, with tightening of central control, and the resulting restriction of spending, using an arbitrary standard set by officials in Whitehall.

Local councils' ability to realise the objectives for which they were elected was deliberately undermined, and the end result was the abolition of the GLC and other metropolitan authorities, and the punishment of councillors who had defied government in pushing ahead with housing and other essential services endorsed by their electorates. The proof of the democratic accountability of the councils who defied the government's edicts lay in their continued re-election despite the attacks to which they were subjected.

The Bill proposes that there should be no limits on local councillors other than prosecution for corruption and subjection to re-election.

The job of the police is notionally to 'keep the Queen's Peace', a way of protecting police forces from the influence of politicians (save the Home Secretary who has statutory responsibilities.) Since the police exist to ensure law and order and to protect us and not control us, the Bill increases their accountability to local communities by giving local authorities the power to appoint and dismiss the Chief Constable and require that guidelines be agreed between the police and these councils.

The principle of 'building block democracy' would mean that the diverse needs and aspirations of people throughout the country would be met locally by conscious political acts, and the electors could witness democracy in action in the effects of the votes cast on policies.

The accountability of all power

The second principle of the Bill follows directly from the first – that wherever possible, all those with political power should be elected democratically and made accountable for their actions.

Election entrenches the idea of accountability, and the Freedom of Information clause in the Bill could guarantee that the effect of decisions made by those who had been elected would be more widely known to the electors: strengthening greatly the democratic process.

Ministers responsible for Scottish affairs and Welsh affairs would be elected by the Scottish and Welsh electorates and sit in their own parliaments, not as at present appointed from among MPs of a party in government which might be unrepresentative of those electorates.

The House of Lords would be swept away and replaced by an elected House of the People, with a representation proportionate to the population of the three countries – *i.e.* a second chamber operating on the basis of consent not inheritance or appointment.

The Council of State, which would replace the secretive Privy Council, would be entrusted with certain powers subject to Parliament and would derive its authority *from* Parliament, not from the accumulated ministerial appointments to cabinet and other positions which make up the current moribund body. Moribund though it appears, in a national emergency the Privy Council has certain powers to govern the country by Orders in Council, potentially a most important role, which would be exercised by the new Council of State accountable to Parliament.

Similarly, a President would be elected by Parliament and replace the Crown for all formal purposes. But the President would be removable in a way that the current head of state is not. All the prerogative powers associated with the Crown would be transferred to Parliament so that statute law was substituted for the arbitrary administrative acts of the Queen's First Minister.

The concept of a President, acting primarily as head of state, accords with our political traditions and it is not intended to introduce a presidential system as in France or America where executive power is highly personal and focused in one individual elected by the people. The comparison here is more with Switzerland, Austria or Ireland than with France or America.

The purpose of this new constitution is to work with and not against the grain of our political experience; we have for years been familiar with a head of state who literally presides and such a President would play a much more familiar part than the adoption of an executive president.

Candidates for the presidency would be drawn from the elected representatives and would remain subject to the ultimate authority of Parliament. The President would be comparable in his or her election to the current Speaker, whose accountability to the whole of Parliament would guarantee that no President could usurp executive powers.

The End of the Monarchy

It follows that the monarchy, as a legal institution, could have no place in such a democracy and the Bill ends its legal status, leaving the Queen as a private citizen with all the rights and duties that flow from that status.

No Bill that affects the royal prerogative can currently be debated without the prior consent of the monarch. The Commonwealth of Britain Bill therefore had to be sent to Buckingham Palace through the Home Secretary to obtain the Queen's consent to it being presented to the Commons.

The request for permission from the monarch to debate a measure that would end the monarchy, poses some interesting questions for the Sovereign. If permission were to be refused, the restraints on parliamentary democracy would be exposed; if permission is granted then it is possible to argue that the monarch has no objection to the passage of the Bill and the abolition of the monarchy. In actual fact, Royal Consent was obtained for this Bill and is reproduced here.

The House of Commons clerks have advised that there is no legal reason why the Bill should not be carried through under the provisions of the Parliament Act of 1911, which allow the Commons to override the Lords. Theoretically therefore it is only a majority of Members of Parliament who prop up the monarchy, which it is in their power to end had they the will to do so, and it could be effected under the provisions of this Bill after its passage and the Referendum to establish it.

The establishment of a Commonwealth of Britain would, of course, liberate the Royal Family from the burdensome duties and severe statutory restrictions which now apply to the monarch and all her heirs.

They are required to be members of the Anglican communion, and would be disqualified at once from royal succession if they left the church, joined any other denomination or became theists or agnostics.

It would be quite wrong for any campaign to end the monarchy to degenerate into a personal attack upon the Royal Family; they did not choose the job, and occupy

COMMON SENSE

QUEEN ANNE'S GATE
LONDON SW1H 9AT

25 June 1991

Dn Tony,

    You asked me to seek The Queen's Consent to your Commonwealth of Britain Bill and I undertook to write to you when the outcome was known.

    I have now been advised that Her Majesty has been pleased to place Her Prerogative and Interest, so far as they may be affected by the Bill, at the disposal of Parliament for the purpose of the Bill.

Yours sincerely,

The Rt Hon Tony Benn, MP.
House of Commons
LONDON, S.W.1.

their positions as a result literally of the accident of birth. Parliament might wish to award the Queen some compensation for loss of office.

Parliamentary control of foreign affairs, defence and the security services

It follows from these changes that all the Crown prerogatives now exercised unaccountably would fall to the new Parliament to administer, and amongst the most important would be those which dealt with foreign affairs, defence and the security services.

In a political situation in which domestic and foreign affairs overlap so much that a distinction is impossible and meaningless, control of the prerogatives could be crucial to greater democratic control of government policy.

In practice, this would mean that all laws assented to by British ministers at the European Community tables would be subject to prior assent by Parliament and could subsequently be repealed by the British Parliament, where domestic laws would take priority over European ones in the case of conflict.

Also, British representatives at the United Nations would have to be elected by the House of Commons and no veto could be cast at the UN without the approval of that House. No foreign forces could be stationed here without the specific consent of the House of Commons and all treaties would need to be ratified by the House, which is not at present a legal requirement.

Under the parliamentary control of the prerogatives, the security services would be made accountable to the Commons and subject to an annual report and renewal of their powers, a system which operates for the armed forces in general. This would be an additional safeguard against individuals or groups antagonistic to the interests of the elected government.

The Official Secrets Acts would be repealed and with certain restrictions for a very limited range of subjects all government information could be made publicly available immediately. This is an essential provision if the knowledge necessary for the workings of a mature democracy is to be available to those with electoral power.

Equal representation for women

The principle in the Bill of equal representation of women and men in all the parliaments – Commonwealth, English, Scottish, Welsh – and local authorities introduces a new and important departure and requires special consideration.

Women are a majority in the population but their present representation on all elected bodies bears no numerical relationship to that fact. For many centuries women were explicitly excluded from voting and therefore from sitting in the Commons, and the struggle to change this was long and difficult.

Unless specific action is taken, this defect in representation will *never* be corrected for all sorts of social, institutional and cultural reasons. The remedy proposed in recent years is that there should be some 'quota' for women. This concept implies that women are part of a minority, a complete misunderstanding of the whole issue. It also sets up a tension between women and men which is both damaging and unnecessary.

We have long accepted the idea of geographical representation whereby each constituency has its own MP; such a system guarantees some spread of interests of different areas.

The Bill adopts the principle of gender representation and each constituency would elect two MPs, one a man and one a women, with all electors having a vote for both.

The point about gender is that while men and women may be black, white, Asian, Christian, Muslim, atheist and sometimes a combination of these, they are *either* men *or* women. There is no justification for the discrimination against women of whatever colour or creed or religion other than that it has been a historical fact.

It would be necessary to reorganise constituencies – possibly to reduce the number by half – but in any case since so many of the powers of the present House of Commons would be devolved to other bodies, this might be quite sensible.

Such an arrangement would introduce an element of proportionality; it would be possible for electors to vote for candidates of differing parties by voting for a man from one party and a woman from another, while retaining the local link that is essential if parliamentary representation is to retain its geographical element.

Such a change would transform the whole nature of all the assemblies, the issues that came up for consideration, the nature possibly of the chambers, without embittering the relationship between men and women.

Votes at sixteen

The voting age was reduced to 18 in 1969 and despite great debate at the time it has been generally accepted without regret. There can be no reason why those who are old enough to marry, to work (if they can find a job) and to pay taxes and may additionally join the armed forces and be called upon to fight for their country, should be excluded from the right to vote.

If young people are expected to obey laws they should also be able to participate in making them.

Voting by residence qualification

At present the right to vote is limited to British citizens who have a residential qualification, and those citizens who have lived abroad for not more than 25 years.

Such arrangements do not stand close examination: a 'foreigner' may have lived and worked in Britain for most of his or her life and paid taxes here but is excluded from any right to participate in the political process; by contrast, someone who has British nationality but has lived abroad for years can still vote.

The simplest and best way in the Bill of dealing with this anomaly is to make residence the only qualification with special provision for the homeless.

Oaths

The Bill removes all present oaths of allegiance to the Crown by a single oath to uphold the constitution; this would be taken by everybody in authority from the President to ministers and MPs, magistrates and mayors, officers and civil servants; everyone, that is, except Anglican priests since the church would be disestablished and would have no state duties.

Such an oath would be legally binding and would provide some guarantee that those in power or positions of authority would be personally responsible for the discharge of the responsibility conferred on them in whatever capacity they took the oath.

The separation of church and state

Since the Church of England was nationalized by King Henry VIII, in conflict with the Pope to bring it under his personal authority, the ending of the monarchy would necessarily end the relationship between monarch and established church. The prayers read at the beginning of every day's sitting of Parliament reveal in their language and philosophy the extent of that relationship.

It is unique to England that the established church remains, and nowhere else in the world-wide Anglican communion do these arrangements exist. The church in Scotland is not under the control of the state and in Wales it has already been disestablished.

It is absurd that a Prime Minister and Parliament whose members do not have to be Christians, let alone Anglicans, should have any responsibility for the appointment of bishops, or changes to the prayer book, or for any administration of the Church of England; not only is it ludicrous, but it is also undemocratic since it denies the church the right to determine its own administration or choose its own leaders.

Moreover the Church of England is a minority faith in this country and there are many other Christian denominations and indeed other religions existing here, not to mention the majority of people who do not practise any faith and may be humanists, atheists or agnostics.

All religions, and those who do not hold or practise any faith, are entitled to equal treatment under the law. But the blasphemy laws, which protect only the Church of England and its doctrines, are a standing insult to those of other faiths and none, as the anger of Muslims in the Salman Rushdie case proved.

The Bill would liberate the church and because the House of Lords will disappear anyway, the removal of Church of England bishops who currently sit in it would be automatic. Likewise, the role of the archbishops at the coronation ceremony would also disappear, along with that ceremony.

PRAYERS FOR THE PARLIAMENT

O LORD our heavenly Father, high and mighty, King of kings, Lord of lords, the only Ruler of princes, who dost from thy throne behold all the dwellers upon earth; Most heartily we beseech thee with thy favour to behold our most Gracious Sovereign Lady Queen ELIZABETH, and so replenish her with the grace of thy Holy Spirit, that she may alway incline to thy will, and walk in thy way: Endue her plenteously with heavenly gifts, grant her in health and wealth long to live, strengthen her that she may vanquish and overcome all her enemies; and finally after this life she may attain everlasting joy and felicity, through Jesus Christ our Lord. *Amen.*

ALMIGHTY God, by whom alone Kings reign, and Princes decree justice; and from whom alone cometh all counsel, wisdom, and understanding; We thine unworthy servants, here gathered together in thy Name, do most humbly beseech thee to send down thy Heavenly Wisdom from above, to direct and guide us in all our consultations: and grant that, we having thy fear always before our eyes, and laying aside all private interests, prejudices, and partial affections, the result of all our counsels may be to the glory of thy blessed Name, the maintenance of true Religion and Justice, the safety, honour, and happiness of the Queen, the publick wealth, peace and tranquillity of the Realm, and the uniting and knitting together of the hearts of all persons and estates within the same, in true Christian Love and charity one towards another, through Jesus Christ our Lord and Saviour. *Amen.*

The establishment of the Church of England has long been an anomaly and its irrelevance is widely accepted by the church itself, so that this change would be the natural development of changes that have steadily altered the relationship of church and state over the centuries. Far from weakening the church, as has been argued, it would be likely to increase its influence in future, freed from the shackles of state control.

Ending patronage

One of the most corrupting elements in the hierarchical system of British government is the number and range of appointments that flow from the Crown, the powers for which are exercised by the Prime Minister and other ministers. All personal titles and ranks would cease.

The powers over the creation of peers would automatically disappear with the ending of the House of Lords, but the Prime Minister is also in control of honours for large numbers of people and, since there are always ten times as many people who hope to receive honours as actually get them, the penumbra of patronage extends far and wide.

Disestablishment of the church would, of course end all ecclesiastical patronage, and the provision that all high court appointments must be confirmed by Parliament would limit its operation in the legal profession.

The Referendum

Changes of the magnitude set out in the Bill could only be carried through by popular consent; this is provided for by the introduction of a referendum of ratification which would be held after the present Parliament had debated and passed the Bill, a referendum offering a choice on the voting system to be adopted.

Subsequent changes to the new constitution would also have to be ratified by referendum, and this would be the ultimate safeguard against any seizure of power or coup, because the courts would be required to abide by the new constitution, unlike at present when courts are compelled to uphold all decisions of the Crown, including a dissolution of Parliament and dismissal of a Prime Minister with a parliamentary majority.

A Commonwealth for Europe

The future of Europe is of great concern to the people of this country after its involvement in two bloody world wars fought on that continent, and their ideological aftermath. From the Russian Revolution in 1917 to the fall of the communist system in 1991 the European continent has been divided primarily on ideological grounds, with fascism dominant for much of the 1930s followed by the Cold War period after the second war.

These conditions gave rise to the establishment of the European Economic Community and to the North Atlantic Treaty Organization, both of which were committed to preserving capitalism and defending it from external attack. Politically, the progress towards a federal Europe has continued apace, from the Messina Conference of 1955 to the Edinburgh summit in 1992, and the final stages of a full union forecast at Maastricht, complete with a common currency and an independent central bank, would remove economic policy effectively from the constituent governments.

The many nations not in the new union will be cut of from these developments and this means that the continent is likely to remain divided for a very long time ahead.

There are too many international links and common interests binding the nations of Europe together, and too great a danger from old nationalisms, for us to want to risk a return to former insularity.

But those who argue for this, denounced as 'Little Englanders', could not properly be described as anti-European, since cooperation does not hang upon the close integration of the kind built up in Europe over the years.

Inter-governmental negotiations are the traditional way of countries working together and Britain's relations with the United States, the Commonwealth countries and other nations under that system have not been unsuccessful.

Federal Union or Commonwealth?

There *are* alternatives to a bureaucratic, centralised, political Union of Europe. A democratic federation, comparable to the United States of America, with its House of Representatives, Senate and President and Vice-President elected by the population could not be faulted on democratic grounds since it would mean the abolition of the Commission, and the central bank would become accountable as the Federal Reserve Bank is in the United States. But this is the very opposite of the arrangements existing under the Maastricht Treaty, and advocates of European political union do not want, or believe in, this alternative.

Whereas the United States is committed by its constitution to the principles of 'life, liberty and the pursuit of happiness', the European Union is committed to the maintenance of capitalism, and the European Parliament has little or no power over the ministers from every country who meet to legislate in secret, but who can only act on proposals initiated by the Brussels Commission.

It is inconceivable that Americans would endorse the sort of constitution that has been devised for the new Europe.

To argue for a straightforward trans-Atlantic transplant from the US to Europe might be unlikely, but it could not be said to amount to an anti-European position.

The concept of a Commonwealth of Europe is quite distinct from a Union or fully-fledged American-style federation, because it seeks to harmonise the policies of the continent on the basis of consent, at the pace chosen by each country adhering to the Commonwealth, of which there would be over fifty.

The Bill argues for close cooperation, but rejects the Treaty of Rome as too centralised and sets out new objectives; including ever-closer association for the welfare of all, based upon the maintenance of mutual respect for self-governing status and emphasising the inter-governmental nature of the cooperation.

It would commit members to the Charter of the United Nations and to the need to preserve the cultural, political, economic, religious and institutional identity of all the member states, calling for good-will and tolerance.

The Commonwealth would need to have its own institutions including an Assembly, a council of ministers, a court of justice, a human rights commission and a secretariat but they would have no power to take action that would prejudice the democratic decisions of the member states, although membership of the Commonwealth could be suspended.

The membership of the Commonwealth would be open to all states that lie within the continent, and any could leave the commonwealth.

The Assembly would have as its main function the drafting of conventions which once ratified by the council of ministers would be transmitted to the member states; areas of harmonisation would include food, energy, trade, social and political, environmental, international and defence.

But the key difference between the Commonwealth and a Union would be that law making would remain the exclusive function of the member states, which would be obliged to try to comply with these conventions, subject to the consent of their own Parliaments and electors.

The United Nations is an organisation with a long tradition of a similar kind of cooperative work.

The dangers of a full Union are extremely serious. Union is supposed to prevent the growth of the worst kind of nationalism. But under the Maastricht Treaty the electors in every country would discover that they were being deprived of any influence over the laws governing them. This feeling of disenfranchisement could turn the blame for industrial and social problems towards other nations in the Union rather than on the nature of the Union itself.

Communism run from Moscow broke down because it was bureaucratic, inefficient and inflexible; and there is a real risk that capitalism run from Brussels or Frankfurt might reproduce the same sense of frustration and anger, as undemocratic institutions become more powerful and less responsive. Community bureaucracy is already a nightmare.

The chaos that followed the dissolution of both the old Soviet Union and the Yugoslavia federation is a sober lesson not to fall into the same trap in Europe. By seeking to harmonize by consent, at the pace appropriate in each country, these dangers might be averted.

Technocratic centralism

The new technologies of the 20th century have been used to justify escalating centralisation of power.

COMMON SENSE

Under the Cold War command economy, the Soviet
Union's economic decisions were, we were told, taken
centrally, unlike our own market economy; but unawares, a
similar process was taking place in the west among multinational companies, banks and in the military-industrial
complex and space programmes.

The overall control of the capitalist economy has been
different, but capitalism was greatly influenced by movements in the international money markets that were completely exempt from any democratic control. The
stockbrokers and currency speculators of New York or
London can properly be compared to the party appa-
ratchiks in Moscow and Leningrad.

Nowhere is this convergence clearer than in the military
sphere where the complexity, cost and dangers of modern
military systems, and the supposed threat from real or
imagined enemies, had been used by both blocs to establish
immensely powerful and centralised systems.

The similarities between these economic and political
systems should not obscure differences, but they share an
element of distrust of democracy in respect of the running
of their industrial and economic systems and in their
approach to the media. With the ending of the Cold War,
the west has no obvious enemy against whom to mobilise
public opinion, or justification of huge arms expenditure,
and this has caused immense problems. In a capitalist
society the arms programme is the only accepted form of
subsidy for industry, so that when the supposed military
threat eased, that subsidy was cut back, with the promise of
a 'peace dividend'. Capitalism and communism were each
using the other to enforce political loyalty and to justify
central control of ideology and budgets.

If peaceful co-existence was to replace the confrontation
of the Cold War, then it must surely play a central role now
in our thinking about the future of our own continent. The

116

COMMONWEALTH OF BRITAIN AND EUROPE

Commonwealth of Europe Bill is intended to achieve
cooperation built upon the democratic traditions of the
member states.

VI

Conclusion

The whole stable issues forth such a stench that is intolerable; and it will become more than the work of a day to cleanse it. Prepare your brooms, fellow countrymen, make them of the toughest birch, and you shall finally succeed.
                                       Richard Carlile, 1820

The status quo is comfortable. The social pecking order is well-established. The familiar can give a sense of security even to those who have been left out of the social system.

Those who benefit from the status quo have every reason to persuade the rest that it would be better to leave things as they are than risk the uncertainty of a system devoid of the old accepted procedures.

And since the same ideology motivates the mass communicators, those who advocate reform are seen as troublemakers or dreamers who do not have the true interest of the nation at heart. This deeply conservative philosophy ignores all the facts that point in the other direction and therefore its exponents lose touch with reality, or have to attempt to suppress it.

118

CONCLUSION

Nowhere is this more evident than in the aura which surrounds our system of monarchical government, which is sustained by lack of any serious analysis of how it really works and in whose interests.

The degree of official self-deception promulgated to persuade the populace that Britain's constitution is the envy of every other country is breath-taking and it is no longer believed either by those who deliver the message or those who receive it.

The defects are mainly well understood at the very top, but in general criticism is dealt with by discouraging discussion but allowing a few minor adjustments and window dressing operations, like the most recent one relating to the honours system.

Against this background a number of changes in constitutional practice have come to be advocated by groups composed of people close to the centre of power, changes which recognise that public support for the present system is weakening. Such groups advocate reform of the voting system, a Bill of Rights which elevates judges above Parliament, and a closer integration of Britain into a European Union.

These ideas, however radical they sound, would have the effect of centralising power even more strongly, and would move decision-making away from the electors and the MPs to unaccountable officials and administrators.

Even proportional representation in its purest form, using the national list system, would have the effect of transferring power from the local parties and constituencies which now select, elect and de-select candidates, into the hands of party leaders who would gain greater patronage than they already enjoy, and would be free to make deals with other parties to gain office for themselves.

That is the route to a National Government, or one-party

state, which would deny voters a choice of policies and is one reason why the idea finds favour with some influential people who, sensing the magnitude of the economic and political crisis, fear that it might lead to the election of a government of a kind that would challenge their privileges, and to some changes that might erode their powers.

Those who advocate such reform believe that the problem lies with the legislature and not the executive, which they actually want to strengthen. This is the very opposite view to those who fought for political power through Parliament and saw the House of Commons as a means by which the people might be able to control the executive and act as a countervailing force to the huge accumulation of private power which always supported the executive – and was always supported by the executive in return.

To undermine the House of Commons by subordinating it to judges, commissioners and bankers and paralysing it with endless coalitions though proportional representation would be to undo centuries of struggle by the governed against the governors, and thereby inflict a grave defeat upon the very idea of democracy.

This book, by contrast, has made its starting point a critique from the point of view of those at the base of the pyramid, and not at the peak, and has in consequence come to very different conclusions from those reached by the great and the good.

The greatest threat to authority of whatever kind lies in the possibility that the people might dissent and organise outside the permitted limits; such dissenters have often been dealt with by severe means. This distrust of popular democracy has been at the heart of most systems of government, because rulers, however different their philosophies may be, and by whatever means they have acquired their power, have one thing in common – their determination to retain that power at all costs.

But inevitably this deep suspicion of the people and of democracy itself has fed the causes of civil disorder and war, because the peaceful means to change have been blocked, leaving no alternative to violent revolt.

Although separatism, parochialism, and petty national- ism may appear to be the main beneficiaries of pressure for justice and democracy, leading to racism and xenophobia and bloody conflict, such movements might be interpreted as a quite legitimate desire to bring decision-making down to a more accessible level and away from remote, imper- sonal and uncaring rulers who determine the lives of people.

In that sense such movements reflect a demand for greater democracy and should be accommodated rather than ritually denounced.

In a world that has shrunk to a mere village by the development of communications technology, decisions affecting the survival of the planet as a whole will have to be taken at the global level, but the scope of that decision- making will need to be restricted to safeguarding humanity.

It is in this context that consideration needs to be given to the reform of the United Nations as the world enters the new century; and the demand for the democratic control of political, economic and military power on a global scale is widely accepted as imperative to protect human rights, assist disarmament and development and defend the envi- ronment and the wild-life of the planet.

At the time the UN was formed, no-one foresaw that the anti-colonial movements would succeed so quickly to free their countries from the imperial yoke and to enable them to become full members of the organisation alongside their old masters.

The Cold War and the anti-colonial struggle gave birth to the Non-Aligned Movement of over a hundred of the newly independent states, whose influence was beginning to be felt but who lacked the economic and military power of the members of the Security Council and other more industrialised nations.

The end of the Soviet Union meant the return of a new imperialism, dressing itself up in the UN flag, but actually reflecting the overwhelming power of the United States which was determined to fill the power vacuum.

Such a development must not be allowed to go on unchecked and it is essential that the United Nations be reformed to take account of the needs of the rest of the developing world.

The Commonwealth of Britain Bill challenges the powers of the British government to take its seat at the UN by the sole use of the royal prerogative and substitutes the authority of the Commons; other elected legislatures in the world will have to hold their own ministers accountable for their votes there.

There are practical as well as moral reasons for demanding greater democracy, for no system of government can hope to survive over a long period without a high and continuing degree of consent.

If that consent is neither valued nor sought, nor alternative views permitted, the build up of public hostility may be so strong that a system will collapse or be overthrown, as has occurred many times in the past. And when force is used to overthrow an authoritarian regime it is almost inevitable that force will continue to be exercised to sustain the successor regime in power, thus denying consent in the new situation as surely as it was in the system it replaced.

This cycle of repression can be witnessed in the old Soviet Union; the overthrow of a tyrannical Tsar led to a dictatorship of the proletariat that itself suppressed dissent, only to be replaced by a new regime that has pledged itself to end that repression, and has began to introduce its own brand of authoritarianism, this time to enforce capitalism.

The same pattern occurred after the victory of post-war anti-colonial movements which often replaced the imperial power with an authoritarian dictatorship of their own.

The second practical argument for consent is the power it gives a people to dismiss a government without bloodshed. It is a formidable achievement which should never be underestimated and even those who are understandingly sceptical about the supposed merits of parliamentary government should not forget the effort made to achieve this right.

This process of centralisation and bureaucratisation in capitalist and communist countries helps explain the European Commission's role, working to an economic philosophy that has acquired the character of a religion. Both capitalism and socialism have spawned a whole set of doctrines to which their followers adhere with a genuinely religious fervour, determined to preserve them intact and equally resolved to exorcise all heretics. Thus the Commission in Brussels resembles the college of cardinals, committed to uphold the authority of Rome (*i.e.* the Treaty), like their episcopal predecessors; and any suffering on the part of those affected by their powers is patiently explained as the price that has to be paid for long-term success (or the after life).

Put in this simple way it is easy to see the real issue, the same as has faced every generation throughout history – namely, how the people can wrench control of their own lives from the powerful.

Appendix 1
The Commonwealth of Britain Bill

Commonwealth of Britain

A
BILL

To establish a democratic, federal and secular Commonwealth of England, Scotland and Wales dedicated to the welfare of all its citizens; to establish fundamental human rights within that Commonwealth; to lower the voting age to 16 years and to make other provision with respect to elections, including equal representation for women; to prescribe a constitutional oath; to establish a Commonwealth Parliament consisting of the House of Commons and the House of the People and to make provision for the term of a Parliament and for legislative and other procedure; to establish the office of President, and a Council of State, and to prescribe the powers of each; to provide for the formation of governments; to amend the law relating to official information, the armed forces and the security services; to make fresh provision for the participation of Britain in the United Nations Organisation and the European Communities; to make the basing of foreign forces in Britain dependent upon the approval of the House of Commons; to make new provision with respect to the judicial system and to establish a National Legal Service; to set up national Parliaments for England, Scotland and Wales; to amend the law relating to local government, the district auditor and the accountability of police forces; to end the constitutional status of the Crown and to make certain consequential provision; to abolish the House of Lords and the Privy Council, to end the recognition in law of personal titles, and to provide for the acknowledgement of service to the community; to disestablish the Church of England, abolish the offence of blasphemy, and to provide for equality under the law for all religions and beliefs; to end British jurisdiction in Northern Ireland; to provide for a Constitution and for constitutional amendment; and to make transitional and related provision.

Presented by Mr Tony Benn

Ordered, by The House of Commons,
to be Printed, 14th December 1992

LONDON: HMSO

Printed in the United Kingdom by HMSO

£4·15 net

Commonwealth of Britain Bill

EXPLANATORY MEMORANDUM

PART I: THE COMMONWEALTH OF BRITAIN

This part of the Bill provides for the establishment of a democratic, secular, federal Commonwealth comprising the Nations of England, Scotland and Wales, dedicated to the maintenance of the welfare of all its citizens.

It establishes a Commissioner for Human Rights and sets out the powers of the courts and of Parliament in maintaining human rights.

The voting age is reduced to 16 and provision is made for all citizens and permanent residents to exercise the vote, excluding citizens who have been permanently resident abroad for more than five years.

It also institutes a new oath to uphold the Constitution to replace the present oaths taken by those in authority.

PART II: THE COMMONWEALTH PARLIAMENT

This Part of the Bill provides for the election of two Houses of Parliament, each to consist of an equal number of men and women, and each to serve for four years.

The House of Commons becomes the supreme legislative authority but the House of the People has certain powers over legislation, the arrangements for which are set out.

It also provides that the laws passed by the Commonwealth Parliament shall take precedence over European Community law where the two conflict.

PART III: THE PRESIDENCY

Provision is made for the election of a President, with certain powers, all of which must be exercised with the consent of the House of Commons.

The role of the President is also set out in respect of the dissolution of Parliament and the issuing of invitations to a person to attempt to form a government.

PART IV: THE COUNCIL OF STATE

This Part provides for the election of a Council of State, to be presided over by the President, half of whose members shall be men and half women, to be elected by the two Houses of Parliament, which shall have certain powers at moments when no government is in power, and all of whose decisions shall be subject to confirmation by the House of Commons.

PART V: THE EXECUTIVE

This Part of the Bill sets out the means by which a government shall be formed and the executive powers which it shall exercise. It also provides for the procedures in the event of the defeat of a government in the House of Commons on a matter of confidence, for its replacement by another administration, and for the exceptional circumstances in which Parliament might be dissolved.

It also provides for freedom of information, and for the accountability of the armed forces and the security services to Parliament.

PART VI: FOREIGN RELATIONS

This Part of the Bill governs the role of Parliament in determining the representation of Britain at the United Nations and in the European Communities, and in controlling foreign forces based in Britain.

PART VII: THE HIGH COURT

This Part of the Bill sets up a High Court, presided over by a Chief Justice, and sets out its responsibilities.

It also makes arrangements for the appointment of judges, after confirmation by Parliament, and for the election of County Court judges and magistrates.

It also establishes a National Legal Service, free at the point of use, for personal litigation.

PART VIII: THE NATIONAL PARLIAMENTS

This Part of the Bill sets up national Parliaments for England, Scotland and Wales, provides for their composition and election and the powers which they exercise through an executive responsible to each national Parliament, subject to the over-riding authority of the Commonwealth Parliament.

PART IX: LOCAL GOVERNMENT

This Part of the Bill, together with Schedule 3, sets out the powers of local authorities and limits the role of the District Auditor.

It also provides for local authority responsibility for police forces.

PART X: THE CROWN

This Part of the Bill ends the constitutional role of the Crown, its heirs and successors and the Crown prerogatives associated with it.

It provides for all Crown lands and property to pass to the State, and for compensation and a pension to be paid to the former Monarch as well as providing for accommodation to be made available for members of the Royal Family.

It confers full civil rights on all members of the Royal family, provides that they should be liable for taxation as are other citizens, and lifts all legal restrictions that now limit the Crown and its successors in respect of their religion or their right to marry whomever they may wish.

It also provides for the abolition of the House of Lords, members of which will be eligible to stand for Parliament; of the Privy Council and of the honours system; and makes alternative arrangements for the recording and rewarding of services to the Commonwealth.

PART XI: RELIGIOUS FREEDOM

This Part of the Bill disestablishes the Church of England, transferring all control of that Church to the General Synod, removes the disqualification of priests to stand for election to the House of Commons, and abolishes the offence of blasphemy.

It accords equal status to all religions and beliefs within the Commonwealth.

PART XII: NORTHERN IRELAND

This Part of the Bill terminates British jurisdiction in Northern Ireland and makes provision for the necessary transitional arrangements.

PART XIII: IMPLEMENTATION

This Part of the Bill describes the process of enactment, the transitional arrangements and the method of amendment of the Constitution, and provides for commencement.

SCHEDULES

Schedule 1: THE CHARTER OF RIGHTS

This Schedule sets out the rights which are to be a part of the Commonwealth Constitution.

Schedule 2: THE CONSTITUTIONAL OATH

This Schedule sets out the words of the Constitutional Oath to be taken by all persons exercising authority in the State.

Schedule 3: ANNUAL REPORT ON THE SECURITY SERVICES

This Schedule sets out the information which the responsible Ministers shall present to Parliament every year.

Schedule 4: THE POWERS OF LOCAL AUTHORITIES

This Schedule sets out the powers which are to be exercised by local authorities.

Commonwealth of Britain Bill

ARRANGEMENT OF CLAUSES

Part XIII

Implementation

Schedules:

BILL

Establish a democratic, federal and secular Commonwealth of   A.D. 1992.
England, Scotland and Wales dedicated to the welfare of all its
citizens; to establish fundamental human rights within that
Commonwealth; to lower the voting age to 16 years and to make
other provision with respect to elections, including equal
representation for women; to prescribe a constitutional oath; to
establish a Commonwealth Parliament consisting of the House
of Commons and the House of the People and to make provision
for the term of a Parliament and for legislative and other
procedure; to establish the office of President, and a Council of
State, and to prescribe the powers of each; to provide for the
formation of governments; to amend the law relating to official
information, the armed forces and the security services; to make
fresh provision for the participation of Britain in the United
Nations Organisation and the European Communities; to make
the basing of foreign forces in Britain dependent upon the
approval of the House of Commons; to make new provision with
respect to the judicial system and to establish a National Legal
Service; to set up national Parliaments for England, Scotland
and Wales; to amend the law relating to local government, the
district auditor and the accountability of police forces; to end the
constitutional status of the Crown and to make certain
consequential provision; to abolish the House of Lords and the
Privy Council, to end the recognition in law of personal titles,
and to provide for the acknowledgement of service to the
community; to disestablish the Church of England, abolish the
offence of blasphemy, and to provide for equality under the law
for all religions and beliefs; to end British jurisdiction in
Northern Ireland; to provide for a Constitution and for
constitutional amendment; and to make transitional and related
provision.

WHEREAS the constitution of the United Kingdom of Great Britain and Northern Ireland has evolved, over the centuries, from its feudal origins, without ever having been systematically examined in terms of its effectiveness in providing democracy or justice for its citizens;

Whereas the accession of the United Kingdom to the Treaty of Rome, and its membership of the North Atlantic Treaty Organisation have transferred to foreign governments and organisations certain sovereign powers which properly belong to the citizens of this country;

Whereas the citizens of the United Kingdom have no legally enforceable human, political, social, legal or economic rights, nor any safeguards against the denial of such rights; and

Whereas it is now urgent that the United Kingdom adopts a new constitution to remedy these and other defects;

Be it therefore enacted, by the Queen's most Excellent Majesty, by and with the advice and consent of the Lords Spiritual and Temporal, and Commons, in this present Parliament assembled, and by the authority of the same, as follows:—

PART I

THE COMMONWEALTH OF BRITAIN

The establishment of the Commonwealth.

1. Britain shall be a democratic, secular, federal Commonwealth, comprising the Nations of England, Scotland and Wales, in association with such islands as have historically been linked to the United Kingdom, to be designated under arrangements made under section 52 below.

The rights of the People.

2.—(1) The Commonwealth shall be dedicated to the maintenance of the welfare of all its citizens, in whom all sovereign power shall be vested, to be exercised by them, and on their behalf, by the representatives whom they shall elect.

(2) Schedule 1 to this Act shall have effect for the purposes of providing for and entrenching certain basic and fundamental human rights.

The Commissioner for Human Rights.

3.—(1) It shall be the duty of the President, the Government and the Courts to use their best endeavours to secure and safeguard these rights.

(2) The House of Commons shall appoint a Human Rights Commissioner, responsible to Parliament ("the Commissioner"), who shall be responsible for monitoring the observance of these rights.

(3) Any person who believes that he or she is being denied his or her rights may petition the Commonwealth Parliament or ask the Human Rights Commissioner to investigate such a complaint, and the Commissioner may examine the claim and submit a report upon it; any such report shall be published, and the House of Commons shall decide upon it within twelve months of publication.

4. The High Court established under section 24 below may undertake judicial review of any administrative act of the Executive, on application of any person complaining of a denial of one or more of the rights set out in Schedule 1 to this Act.

PART I
The Courts and human rights.

5. The House of Commons or the House of the People may review any decision of the High Court if the Human Rights Commissioner has reported that any person has been denied rights as a result of a decision of the Courts, and may pass a resolution requesting the High Court to re-examine the matter, upon which the High Court shall undertake such a re-examination.

Parliament and human rights.

6.—(1) A British citizen who has not been resident abroad for more than the immediately previous five years shall be entitled to register and to vote in all parliamentary and local elections.

The franchise.

(2) A person who has been resident in Britain for more than five years may register and shall have the right to vote in all parliamentary and local elections.

(3) A person who is eligible to vote may exercise that right from the date of that persons's sixteenth birthday.

7. All oaths of allegiance taken by any person to the Crown, or by the Crown on the occasion of the Coronation, and all other oaths taken by any other person in authority, including judges, magistrates, bishops, members of the armed forces or civil service, members of parliament and Privy Counsellors are hereby declared to be null and void, and, where appropriate, are replaced by the words set out in Schedule 2 to this Act.

The Constitutional Oath.

PART II

THE COMMONWEALTH PARLIAMENT

8.—(1) The Commonwealth Parliament—
  (a) shall consist of two Houses, the House of Commons and the House of the People;
  (b) shall be elected for a fixed term of four years; and
  (c) shall not be dissolved before the expiry of that period, unless pursuant to section 17(3) or (4) below.

The establishment of the Commonwealth Parliament.

(2) All elections shall be conducted on the basis of one person one vote from the age of sixteen, and all electors shall be eligible to be candidates, subject only to any disqualification for which the Commonwealth Parliament may provide.

9.—(1) The House of Commons shall—
  (a) decide its procedure;
  (b) elect its Speaker;
  (c) exercise the supreme legislative power; and
  (d) elect the government.

The House of Commons.

(2) The government shall be accountable for all its actions to the House of Commons.

(3) The boundaries of House of Commons constituencies shall
determined on the recommendation of the Boundary Commission und
arrangements made under section 52 below, and each constituency sh
elect one man and one woman to the House of Commons.

The House of the
People.

10.—(1) The House of the People shall be elected in such a way as
represent England, Scotland and Wales in proportion to th
populations.

(2) Half of the members of the House of the People shall be women a
half shall be men.

(3) Further provision for the establishment of the House of the Peo
may be made under section 52 below.

Legislation.

11.—(1) Bills may be introduced into either House of Parliament.

(2) Bills or motions of a character now requiring the consent
recommendation of the Crown shall require the consent
recommendation of the Government before they are proceeded with, b
the House of Commons may, by resolution, proceed with such a bill
motion without that consent or recommendation.

(3) Primary legislation shall be considered by each House in turn.

(4)(a) The House of the People may amend bills brought from t
House of Commons; and

   (b) bills brought from, and amendments made by, the House of t
   People may be accepted or rejected by the House of Commo
   and its decision shall be final.

(5) The House of the People may reject a bill brought from the Hou
of Commons, whereupon the bill shall be returned to the House
Commons which may, after one calendar year has elapsed, again pass t
bill without amendment, in which case the Speaker of the House
Commons shall issue his certificate to that effect and the bill shall
presented to the President for assent forthwith.

(6) The words of enactment of all bills shall be:

   "Be it enacted by the Authority of the President and t
   Commonwealth Parliament, as follows:"

(7) Each statutory instrument passed by the House of Commons sh
be referred to the House of the People, which shall have the power
delay it for a maximum of one month, after which it shall have effe
provided that the House of Commons so further resolves.

The supremacy of
Parliament.

12.—(1) Where legislation passed by the Commonwealth Parliame
conflicts with any directive or regulation issued or approved by t
Council of Ministers or the Commission of the European Communiti
British legislation shall prevail, and shall be so accepted by British cour

(2) Where the House of Commons, by resolution, determines that any directive or regulation of the European Communities should not apply in Britain, such resolution may not be questioned in British courts.

PART III
THE PRESIDENCY

13.—(1) There shall be a President elected from amongst their number, The President. by a two-thirds majority, by both Houses of Parliament sitting together, to serve for a three year term and to be eligible for re-election for one further three year term.

(2) If the office of President is vacant, or the President is unable to discharge the duties of the Presidency, the Speaker of the House of Commons shall act as President until the President is able to discharge the duties of the Presidency or until a new President is elected.

14.—(1)(a) The powers now exercised under Crown prerogative shall Presidential be exercised by the President, who shall act solely upon the advice of the powers. Prime Minister, or of a resolution of the House of Commons (which shall prevail if such resolution is in conflict with the advice of the Prime Minister);

(b) the exercise of such powers shall require the assent of the House of Commons before having effect; and

(c) the powers of the President shall include power—

—to give assent to the passage of legislation;

—to dissolve Parliament;

—to invite a person to attempt to form an administration;

—to make orders for any purpose for which Orders in Council were required before the coming into force of this Act;

—to declare war;

—to order British forces into armed conflict;

—to make peace;

—to recognise foreign governments;

—to sign or ratify treaties;

—to grant pardons;

—to grant charters;

—to make appointments;

—to establish commissions of inquiry;

—to grant commissions in the armed forces;

—to issue orders; and

—to exercise other executive powers not conferred by statute.

(2) Instruments previously made by Order in the Council and which are legislative in character, after being made by the President, shall be brought in as Bills.

(3) Instruments exercising the general administrative powers of the President shall be published and laid before the House of Commons for approval by resolution of that House.

(4) Instruments exercising powers of appointment shall be published, as separate orders for each appointment, and shall be subject to annulment in pursuance of a resolution of the House of Commons.

PART IV

THE COUNCIL OF STATE

Establishment of the Council of State.

15.—(1) There shall be a Council of State consisting of twenty-four persons, of whom twelve shall be men and twelve shall be women.

(2) Half of the members of the Council of State shall be elected by the House of Commons from among its members and half by the House of the People from among its members.

(3) Each member shall serve for a period of two years.

Powers of the Council of State.

16.—(1) In the event of no government being in office, the powers of government shall be vested in the Council of State, and all decisions made by the Council of State shall be subject to confirmation by the House of Commons.

(2) The President shall preside over the Council of State and shall report its decisions to both Houses of Parliament.

PART V

THE EXECUTIVE

The government.

17.—(1) The House of Commons shall, by a simple majority, elect one of its members to form a government as Prime Minister, and that person shall present the Government to the House of Commons for approval as a whole, by resolution, before, he or she takes office.

(2) All executive power shall be vested in the government for so long as it enjoys a majority in the House of Commons, or until the day of first meeting of a new Parliament.

(3) In the event of a government being defeated in the House of Commons on a matter of confidence, the Prime Minister shall tender his or her resignation forthwith to the President who shall consult widely to determine who might best be able to form a new administration, and shall issue an invitation to that person to attempt to do so, and to present his or her govenment to the House of Commons for approval.

(4) Parliament shall be dissolved before the expiry of its term only if—

(a) no person attempting to form a government has secured the approval of the House of Commons for that government:

(b) the President recommends a dissolution: and

(c) the House of Commons votes in favour of a dissolution

and in such a case there shall be a general election to elect a new Parliament for the unexpired term of the previous Parliament.

Freedom of information.
1958. c. 51.

18.—(1) (a) In the Public Records Act 1958 references to "four years" shall be substituted for references to "thirty years".

(b) In section 5(1) of that Act the words from "created" to the end of the subsection, and section 5(2), shall be omitted.

(2) Notwithstanding subsection 1 above, a Minister may certify that a paper should remain secret, and any such certificate shall be laid before the House of Commons for approval by resolution.

(3) The Official Secrets Acts 1911, 1920, 1939 and 1989 are hereby repealed.

(4) All official information shall be published, or made available on request, save that categories of information relating to the following subjects may be protected by order subject to approval by resolution:

    (i) defence and security matters:

    (ii) economic policy:

    (iii) international relations: and

    (iv) personal data:

(5) It shall be a criminal offence to disclose protected information, and penalties and defences shall be specified by an order under section 52 below.

19.—(1) The legal status of all the armed forces of Britain shall depend upon the passing by the House of Commons of an annual authorisation order.

(2) The Chief and Vice-Chief of the Defence Staff, and the Chief of Staff of each of the three Services shall be nominated by the Government and confirmed by the Defence Committee of the House of Commons before they are appointed.

20.—(1) The security services of the Commonwealth shall be accountable to Parliament through the responsible Minister or Ministers, who shall make a report annually to the House of Commons containing the information set out in Schedule 3 to this Act.

(2) The House of Commons may make recommendations by resolution on any aspect of the work of the security services.

(3) The legal status of the security services shall depend upon the passing of an annual authorisation order by the House of Commons.

(4) The head of each security service shall be nominated by the Government and confirmed by the Select Committee of the House of Commons for the time being having responsibility for matters relating to that service.

PART VI

FOREIGN RELATIONS

21.—(1) The British representative attending the Security Council of the United Nations shall be elected by the House of Commons, and shall be removable by a resolution of that House.

(2) No veto may be cast by the British representative on any issue which touches upon the interests of the planet: that is, in respect of proposals for the control of nuclear weapons, chemical weapons or environmental protection, without first having obtained specific approval from both Houses of Parliament.

(3) British delegates to the General Assembly of the United Nations, of whom half shall be men and half shall be women, shall be elected for each session of that organisation, one half by the House of Commons and one half by the House of the People.

The European
Communities.

22.—(1) No vote may be given by a British Minister at the Council of Ministers of the European Communities unless and until the House of Commons has given its approval by resolution to that vote.

(2) The British members of the European Commission shall be nominated by the government and elected by the House of Commons.

(3) A British Commissioner may be removed from his post by a majority vote in both Houses of the Commonwealth Parliament.

Foreign forces in
Britain.

23.—(1) No armed forces of any foreign country, nor any weapons or equipment, shall be

    (a) based in the Commonwealth of Britain or its territorial waters; or

    (b) used from British territory, airspace or territorial waters in any armed conflict

without the prior consent of the House of Commons.

(2) Any treaty which provides for the basing of any foreign forces shall be subject to annual renewal by resolution of the House of Commons at the same time as the annual authorisation orders provided for in section 19 above.

PART VII

THE HIGH COURT

The establishment
of the High Court.

24.—(1) There shall be a High Court, independent of the Commonwealth Government and Parliament.

(2) The High Court shall initially be composed of such persons as are Law Lords and members of the Judicial Committee of the Privy Council at the coming into force of this Act.

(3) The Chair of the High Court shall be known as the Chief Justice of the Commonwealth.

(4) The responsibilities of the High Court shall include the safeguarding of the Commonwealth Constitution and its judgments shall be binding upon the Government.

Judicial
appointments.

25.—(1) Nominations to the High Court shall be made by the President, and shall be confirmed by the Select Committee of the House of Commons for the time being having responsibility for judicial matters, before having effect.

(2) High Court, Appeal Court and County Court judges shall retire when they reach the age of 60.

(3) Members of the High Court and other judges shall be removed only upon a resolution of both Houses of Parliament.

26.—(1) The High Court may nominate persons to serve on a panel from which County Court judges shall be elected by those who are on the electoral register for the House of Commons constituencies which cover the areas for which any such judge is to exercise jurisdiction.

(2) A County Court judge elected under subsection (1) above shall be removed only upon resolution of both Houses of Parliament.

27. Magistrates shall be elected by those who are on the electoral register for the House of Commons constituencies which cover the areas for which any such magistrate is to exercise jurisdiction, shall hold office for four years, and shall be eligible for re-election, up to the age of 60.

Election of magistrates.

28. A National Legal Service shall be established giving to each person the right, free of charge, to be represented in Court on matters of direct personal or family concern, but such a right shall not extend to commercial, industrial or financial enterprises.

National Legal Service.

PART VIII

THE NATIONAL PARLIAMENTS

29.—(1) There shall be national Parliaments elected for England, for Scotland and for Wales.

Establishment of the national Parliaments.

(2) Each Parliament shall decide its own procedure, save that it shall elect its own Speaker, who shall have the same powers in respect of proceedings as the Speaker of the House of Commons.

30.—(1) Half of the Members of each Parliament shall be men and half shall be women.

Composition and election.

(2) National Parliaments shall be elected by those who are registered upon the electoral registers in England, Scotland and Wales respectively, at the same time, and for the same four year period, as the elections for the Commonwealth Parliament, with the exception of any election under section 17(4) above.

31. Each Parliament shall elect its own Executive, which shall hold office for as long as it commands the support of the Parliament to which it is accountable.

The Executives.

32. Each Parliament shall enjoy the power to legislate in all matters save only defence, foreign affairs and Commonwealth finance, which shall remain within the sole authority of the Commonwealth Parliament.

Powers of the national Parliaments.

33. The Commonwealth Parliament may enact legislation applying t the Commonwealth as a whole, and where such enactments conflict wit any enactments of the national Parliaments, the Commonwealt legislation shall have precedence.

PART IX

LOCAL GOVERNMENT

Local government
powers.

34.—(1) Each local authority shall enjoy, in addition to the power conferred by any other enactment, the power to act as it thinks fit i respect of the activities specified in Schedule 4 to this Act.

(2) Nothing in this section shall empower any local authority to tak any action that is explicitly prohibited by Act of Parliament, and if suc an action is taken the Council shall be collectively liable, but no individua councillor shall be personally penalised for that action, excepting onl where he or she may be convicted of any breach of the criminal law.

The District
Auditor.

35.—(1) The powers and duties of the District Auditor shall, in respec of all local authorities, be restricted to

(a) an annual audit of their accounts;

(b) the presentation of that audit to the council of each loca authority, the responsible Minister and to Parliament; and

(c) the making available of accounts at all times for public inspectio in the area covered by each local authority.

(2) The District Auditor shall not have any power to declare an expenditure to be ultra vires, nor to surcharge councillors for decision taken collectively by them in pursuit of their duties as members of th council of a local authority.

Control of the
police.

36. All police forces shall be answerable to the local authorities in th areas which they serve, and shall submit a report annually to thos authorities on the model of the report required by Schedule 4 to this Act

PART X

THE CROWN

The ending of the
constitutional
status of the
Crown.

37. The legal status of the Crown is hereby ended and the Monarch fo the time being, and his or her heirs and successors, shall cease to enjoy, o exercise as Monarch, any political or personal power of any kind, eithe directly through the person of the Monarch, or by prerogative, or throug Ministers.

Crown property.

38. The ownership and control of all Crown lands, buildings an property which are held by the Monarch for the time being, as consequence of his or her occupancy of the Throne, or position as heir t the Throne, shall be transferred forthwith to the Commonwealt Government.

Compensation.

39.—(1) A payment shall be paid from public funds to the perso occupying the Throne at the coming into force of this Act, to dispose o as he or she thinks fit.

(2) A pension shall be paid to the person occupying the Throne at the moment of coming into force of this Act.

(3) Accommodation shall be made available for such members of the Royal family, in such Royal Palaces as may be determined by Parliament.

(4) Provision under this section shall be determined under section 52 below.

40. *All members of the Royal family shall be liable for the payment of taxes and charges paid by a citizen of the Commonwealth, or a person residing in the Commonwealth, as the case may be.*

41.—(1) All restrictions presently imposed by statute or otherwise specifically upon members of the Royal family in respect of their religious faith or in any other way are hereby declared to have no effect.

(2) Members of the Royal family shall enjoy the same rights as those which are enjoyed by any citizen of the Commonwealth, including the right to stand for Parliament.

(3) The Royal Marriages Act 1772 is hereby repealed.

42. The House of Lords is hereby abolished, and from the coming into force of this Act no person shall enjoy any legal status as a Lord Spiritual or Temporal, and any person who was formerly a member of the House of Lords shall enjoy the right to stand for Parliament.

43. The Privy Council, and the style and precedence of Privy Counsellor, are hereby abolished.

44.—(1) No personal title or rank, whether hereditary or not, shall be recognised in law.

(2) No personal title, rank or dignity shall be conferred, nor shall any admission be made to a rank or class of an order of chivalry or any similar order.

(3) The Commonwealth Parliament and the national Parliaments may express gratitude to those citizens who have distinguished themselves through service to the community by Resolutions of Thanks.

(4) Those named in such Resolutions shall receive medals issued under the authority of the Commonwealth Parliament or the appropriate national Parliament.

(5) Nominations for inclusion in Motions for Resolutions of Thanks may be made by any organisation or person; and the selection of those for inclusion in the Motion shall be made each year by a Committee of the House of Commons or of a national Parliament, as the case may be.

PART XI
RELIGIOUS FREEDOM

Disestablishment of the Church of England.

45. The Church of England is hereby disestablished, and all the powers over faith, doctrine, liturgy, property, discipline and appointments now exercised over that Church by the Crown, Parliament or private patrons, shall forthwith be transferred, in their entirety, to the General Synod of the Church of England, to be exercised in accordance with any rules determined by that body.

Abolition of the offence of blasphemy etc.

46.—(1) No proceedings shall be instituted against any person for the offences of blasphemy, blasphemous libel, heresy, schism or atheism.

(2) A person who has been convicted of an offence listed in subsection (1) shall be deemed never to have committed that offence.

Equal status for all religions and beliefs.

47.—(1) Members of all religious denominations, and holders of other beliefs including atheism, agnosticism or humanism, shall have equal status before the law.

1801 c. 63.

(2) The House of Commons (Clergy Disqualification) Act 1801 is hereby repealed, and it is declared that a priest, deacon or minister of the Church of England or any other Christian denomination may stand for election to the House of Commons or the House of the People.

PART XII
NORTHERN IRELAND

Termination of Jurisdiction.

48. Two years after the passage of this Act, or on such earlier date as the Commonwealth Parliament may determine, the jurisdiction of Britain in Northern Ireland shall cease, and from that date no legislation passed by that Parliament shall apply in Northern Ireland.

Arrangements for withdrawal.

49. Orders under section 52 below shall make provision for the withdrawal of all British troops and personnel, and the disposal of premises or equipment which, up to the coming into force of this Act belong to Her Majesty's Government, but no such order shall purport to give powers to make laws or to enforce them in Northern Ireland after the day upon which British jurisdiction ends.

PART XIII
IMPLEMENTATION

The Constitution.

50.—(1) The provisions of this Act shall form a Constitution for the Commonwealth of Britain, subject to approval by referendum.

(2) Within two months of the passing of this Act, an order under section 52 below shall make provision for the holding of a referendum to approve the Constitution.

3) An order mentioned in subsection (2) above shall provide

(a) for the manner of holding the referendum, which shall be conducted on the basis of the Parliamentary constituencies in existence before any new determination under section 9(2);

(b) for the date of the referendum, which shall be held within three months of the passing of this Act;

(c) that approval of the Constitution shall be by simple majority, without requirement as to the total numbers voting;

(d) that the qualification of a voter shall be as set out in section 6 above;

(e) that the referendum shall consult the people on the electoral system under which parliamentary elections shall be conducted, to be decided by a simple majority;

(f) for the manner in which the choice of the people under paragraph (e) above is to be implemented; and

(g) that the referendum shall be held under the overall supervision of the Speaker of the House of Commons, to whom any matter of dispute or doubt shall be referred and whose decision shall be final.

51. After approval in a referendum, the Constitution shall be amended ly with the agreement of both Houses of the Commonwealth rliament and the endorsement of the people in a referendum.

Amendment of the Constitution.

52.—(1) Orders under this section may make further provision as ecified in this Act, or, as necessary, for the implementation of the ovisions of this Act or for transitional purposes.

Further provision under this Act.

(2) Orders under this section shall be laid before the House of mmons by the Prime Minister or by the Speaker.

(3) No order shall be made under this section unless a draft of it has en laid before, and approved by resolution of, the House of Commons.

53. *There shall be defrayed out of money provided by Parliament—*

Expenses.

(a) *any expenses of the Speaker of the House of Commons, or of any Minister, under this Act; and*

(b) *any increase attributable to this Act in the sums so payable out of such moneys under any other Act.*

54.—(1) This Act, except for sections 6, 8(2) and 50, shall come into rce, if approved by referendum as specified in section 50 above, on the y after that approval is announced by the Speaker of the House of mmons.

Commencement and citation.

(2) Sections 6, 8(2) and 50 shall come into force upon the passing of is Act.

(3) This Act may be cited as the Commonwealth of Britain Act 1993.

SCHEDULES

SCHEDULE 1

The Charter of Rights

1. All citizens of Britain shall be entitled to enjoy, and to campaign f universal democratic and enforceable rights, both individual and collecti enshrined in law, adhered to in practice and respected by society, as precondition of self-government and the achievement of full political, social a economic emancipation within a civilized society:

2. Every citizen shall have the following political rights:
   —to freedom of speech;
   —to freedom of assembly and of association for the purpose of expressi an opinion, without interference from the State;
   —to organize for common political, social or economic ends;
   —to practise, or not to practise, any or all religions;
   —to vote in all elections, participate in all electoral processes a institutions, and to contest all elections:
   —to privacy and the protection of personal information a correspondence from surveillance or interference;
   —to information about public, political, social or economic affairs;
   —to freedom of movement, unhindered by arbitrary interference, and to given asylum from political social or economic oppression; and
   —to conscientious objection to service in the armed forces.

3. Every citizen shall have the following legal rights:
   —to personal freedom from arbitrary arrest, detention or harassment;
   —to a fair and impartial hearing by a jury of the citizen's peers if accused any unlawful activity, and to equal treatment before the law and equ access to legal representation;
   —to be presumed innocent until proved guilty, to be informed of all charg laid and the evidence in support of them, and the right to silence court;
   —to freedom from torture or cruel and degrading treatment, and fro capital punishment;
   —to legal advice and services, free at the point of use; and
   —to equal treatment before the law, and in the community, witho discrimination, and regardless of race, sex or sexual preference, colo religious or political conviction or disability.

4. Every citizen shall have the following social rights:
   —to adequate and warm housing and comfortable living conditions;
   —to rest, recreation and leisure, to a limitation of working hours and holidays;
   —to enjoy access to literature, music, the arts and cultural activities;
   —to good health care and preventive medicine, free at the moment of nee
   —to lifelong and free educational provision;
   —to dignity and care in retirement;
   —in the case of women, to control of their own fertility and reproductio
   —to free and equal access to child care;

—to free, effective and equitable means of transportation;

—to a healthy, sustainable, accessible and attractive environment and to clean water and air;

—to media free from governmental or commercial domination; and

—to full access to personal information held by any public authority, subject only to a restriction order signed by a Minister and reported to Parliament.

5. Every citizen shall have the following economic rights:

—to useful work at a fair wage that provides an income sufficient to maintain a decent standard of living;

—to belong to a trade union and to withdraw labour in pursuit of an industrial dispute;

—to participate in all decisions, including those relating to health and safety, affecting the workplace and to information, representation and expression of opinion for all employed persons;

—to full and equal access to all state or social benefits at a level sufficient to meet basic needs; and

—to freedom from taxation in excess of an ability to pay.

SCHEDULE 2

The Constitutional Oath

The Oath under section 7 above shall be in the following terms, and shall be declared in the presence of another person who has taken the Oath, who shall report the names of all those who have taken the Oath before him or her to the President.

"I ... do solemnly declare and affirm that I will be faithful to the Constitution of the Commonwealth of Britain, and will respect its laws, as enacted by Parliament; will preserve inviolably the civil rights and liberties of the people, including the right to self-government, through their elected representatives, and will faithfully and truly declare my mind and opinion on all matters that come before me without fear or favour".

SCHEDULE 3

Annual Report on the Security Services

1. The responsible Minister shall lay before the House of Commons annually a report on the work of the security services setting out the following information:

(a) the total budget of those services, divided into the following categories:

    (i) wages and salaries;

    (ii) equipment and offices;

    (iii) expenditure in Britain; and

    (iv) expenditure abroad

(b) the total number of persons employed directly and on contract;

(c) the total number of names held in records kept in any form by the service in question;

(d) the number of telephones intercepted, by any means, during the course of the previous year;

(e) the number of persons whose mail was intercepted and opened for examination;

(f) the broad categories under which interceptions mentioned i paragraphs (d) or (e) above were made;

(g) the number of arrests made and convictions obtained as a result of suc interceptions; and

(h) the nature of the suspected crimes or subversive or other activitie considered to justify such interceptions.

2. (a) A draft order to renew authority for the legal status of the securit services shall be laid together with the report required by section 20 of this Ac and this Schedule, and shall be amendable.

(b) The authority for the legal status of the security services shall lapse si months after the laying of a draft order under sub-paragraph (a) above if th draft order has not previously been approved by resolution of the House o Commons.

SCHEDULE 4

POWERS OF LOCAL AUTHORITIES

1. The powers of local authorities shall include any activity, not explicitl prohibited by law, which that authority believes to be in the interests of th people in its area, including the powers:

— to provide any service, and to finance such a service, or other activit out of any income accruing to the authority, or by borrowing;

— to acquire by purchase, or to hold, any land, buildings or other propert or shares in any company;

— to establish any company, either wholly owned by the authority, o jointly with others, to undertake any task authorised by the authorit

— to assist by way of grant, loan subsidy or the acquisition of equity, an commercial undertaking;

— to make grants to any voluntary body, whatever the nature of the servic that that body may provide, under any arrangements that it thinks fi

— to provide a service of news and information, by whatever mean appears to the authority to be appropriate, so that the people may hav access to accurate news, free from bias or distortion, with a diversity o views, such a service to extend to the use of posters, leaflet newspapers, magazines, radio, television or video broadcast and th means of distribution thereof; and

— to give, after consultation with that body, an instruction to any publi body or service operating in the authority's area to desist from an action, which, in the opinion of the authority, is damaging to th interests of the people living in the area, or to request the replacemen of any official employed by such an authority, whose actions have ha a similar effect, such instruction or request to become effective after s months, unless the House of Commons, on motion of the responsibl Minister, resolves that such an instruction or request is contrary to th national interest.

Appendix 2
The Commonwealth of Europe Bill

Commonwealth of Europe

A
BILL

To provide for the establishment of a Commonwealth
of Europe, and for purposes connected therewith.

Presented by Mr Tony Benn

Ordered, by The House of Commons,
to be Printed, 17th *June* 1992

LONDON: HMSO

Printed in the United Kingdom by HMSO

£2·30 net

A

B I L L

TO

Provide for the establishment of a Commonwealth of Europe, and A.D. for purposes connected therewith.

WHEREAS it would be in the interests of the people of the United Kingdom to co-operate closely with the people in all the other countries in the continent of Europe for the welfare of all, and

Whereas the European Community set up under the Treaty of Rome has conferred too much political power on the Commission, which is not elected, nor can it be removed by democratic means, and

Whereas the Community laws, which take precedence over the domestic laws of member states, are made by the Council of Ministers, in secret, without requiring the prior consent of the elected parliaments of member states, and

Whereas the proposals for an economic, monetary and political union contained in the Treaty of Maastricht would necessarily undermine still further the democratic accountability of those with power to those over whom that power would be exercised, and

Whereas the effect of this would be to weaken the rights of the peoples of Europe to determine the policies of those in power, and

Whereas the long-term effect of these changes could be to lead to apathy, or the recrudescence of the worst form of nationalism, and

Whereas great new opportunities now exist for the creation of a wider European system, based upon the progressive harmonization of interests between the fully self-governing states in the continent;

Now therefore be it enacted, and it is hereby enacted by the Queen's Most Excellent Majesty, by and with the advice and consent of the Lords Spiritual and Temporal, and Commons, in this present Parliament assembled, and by the authority of the same, as follows:—

1. Within six months of the passing of this Act, Her Majesty's Government shall summon a Conference in London of the governments of all the European States listed in the Schedule to this Act, to be held not less than six months thereafter, to discuss the establishment of a Commonwealth of Europe, to which all nations in Europe should be invited to adhere.

2. At the Conference referred to in section 1 above, the draft of a Treaty of London, in the form set out in the Schedule to this Act, shall be presented to the Conference for discussion, amendment and subsequent ratification by the processes that apply for that purpose in each of the nations willing to participate.

3. Notwithstanding section 2 of the European Communities Act 1972, all legislation that has been enacted, or may be enacted by the United Kingdom Parliament, or legislation made under the authority of the United Kingdom Parliament shall, from the passing of this Act, have precedence over any laws, directives or regulations of the European Community.

4. *There shall be paid out of money provided by Parliament any expenses of any Minister under this Act.*

5. This Act may be cited as the Commonwealth of Europe Act 1992.

SCHEDULE

THE TREATY OF LONDON

For the establishment of a

COMMONWEALTH OF EUROPE

PREAMBLE

WE:

The duly elected representatives of the following nations representing the peoples of Europe:

Albania
Andorra
Armenia
Austria
Azerbaijan
Belgium
Belorussia
Bosnia-Herzegovina
Bulgaria
Croatia
Cyprus
Czechoslovakia
Denmark
Eire
Estonia
Finland
France
Georgia
Germany
Greece
Hungary
Iceland
Italy
Kazakhstan
Kyrgyzstan
Latvia
Liechtenstein
Lithuania
Luxembourg
Malta
Moldavia
Monaco
The Netherlands
Norway
Poland
Portugal
Romania
Russia
San Marino
Slovenia
Spain
Sweden
The Swiss Confederation
Tajikistan
Turkey
Turkmenistan
Ukraine

The United Kingdom
Uzbekistan
The Vatican City State

DETERMINED to lay the foundation of an ever-closer association of the peoples of Europe for the common welfare of them all;

ACCEPTING that this association must be based upon the maintenance of mutual respect for the fully self-governing status of all the signatories of this Treaty;

RESOLVED to work for the fullest degree of co-operation between the governments here represented in all matters that concern the continent as a whole, and its relations with the rest of the world community;

COMMITTED to uphold the Charter of the United Nations and its decisions, and to the promotion of peace, democracy, disarmament and development and the maintenance and extension of Human Rights as specified in the United Nations Declaration of Human Rights;

BELIEVING that the rich and diverse cultural, political, economic, religious and institutional identity of Member States must be preserved inviolate if peace and progress are to be achieved;

RESOLVED to work for these ends with good-will and in a spirit of tolerance and understanding;

HAVE DECIDED, at our meeting in London, to create a Commonwealth of Europe, to which all entitled Nations may adhere, and which shall be in accordance with the following provisions:—

Article 1

By this Treaty, the High Contracting Parties establish amongst themselves a COMMONWEALTH OF EUROPEAN NATIONS.

Article 2

The Commonwealth of Europe shall assume the task of working, by common consent, for the harmonious and peaceful development of all Member States, and the welfare of all the people living in them, and of the continent as a whole.

Article 3

The tasks entrusted to the Commonwealth shall be carried out by the following institutions:
    The Assembly
    The Council of Ministers
    The Court of Justice
    The Human Rights Commission
    The Secretariat.

Each institution shall act strictly within the limits of the powers conferred upon it by this Treaty.

Article 4

Member States shall undertake to promote appropriate measures, whether general or particular, to win support from their own parliaments to secure fulfilment of the obligations arising out of this Treaty, or resulting from recommendations made by the institutions of the Commonwealth.

Article 5

Member States shall, in cooperation with the institutions of the Commonwealth, seek to use their best efforts to harmonize their policies.

Article 6

The institutions of the Commonwealth shall take no action that would prejudice the interests of any Member State, or its fully self-governing status.

Article 7

Any independent Nation whose frontiers lie partly, or wholly, within the Continent of Europe shall be eligible to join the Commonwealth, subject only to the consent of a majority of the Members of the Assembly.

Article 8

Any Member State shall be free to leave, after giving twelve months' notice to the Secretariat.

Article 9

The Assembly may suspend the membership of any Member State by a simple majority vote, and may extend, or lift, that suspension at any time.

Article 10

This Treaty shall remain in force for an indefinite period, unless a majority of the Assembly, and of the Council of Ministers, recommend that it be terminated.

Article 11

This Treaty shall come into force when it has been ratified by the National Parliaments of a majority of the Nations whose representatives have signed it, and when a majority of the peoples of those Nations have approved it by a simple majority in referenda in their respective countries.

THE INSTITUTIONS

Article 12

THE ASSEMBLY

The Assembly shall be composed of a maximum of five hundred Members, and of men and women in equal numbers; and the representation of each Member State shall reflect the proportion which its population represents of the total population of Member States; save that in calculating such representation fractions shall be disregarded, provided always that a Member State shall have at least two representatives.

It shall be elected for a four year term, on the basis of an electoral system to be chosen by each Member State, provided that there shall be a single polling day within three months of the coming into force of this Treaty.

It shall meet in public and shall have the responsibility for determining the policy of the Commonwealth as a whole, subject to the limitations set down in the Preamble to this Treaty.

It shall elect its own presiding officer each year, may determine its own procedure and shall have power to establish its own Committees.

Its Members shall be paid out of the national budgets of the Member States, as determined by each of them severally.

Its functions shall include the drafting of Conventions on any matter the Assembly deems to be necessary, which shall then be transmitted to the Council of Ministers and all Member States for ratification.

Article 13

THE COUNCIL OF MINISTERS

The Council of Ministers shall be composed of one representative from the government of each Member State.

It shall meet in public, unless, by a majority, it decides that it is in the interests of the Commonwealth, as a whole, that certain matters should be discussed privately, and it shall publish all the decisions which it has taken, as soon as practicable.

Thereafter, it shall consider recommendations of the Assembly, and shall make recommendations to the governments of Member States.

The Council shall be charged with the task of actively seeking to harmonize the policies of all the nations of the Commonwealth on any issue which concerns the continent as a whole, including the following matters:
> Economic and Industrial
> Food and Agriculture
> Energy
> Trade
> Political
> Social
> Environmental
> International policy
> Defence and Disarmament
> Development.

Article 14

THE COURT OF JUSTICE

A Court of Justice shall be established, composed of judges nominated by each Member State, and confirmed by the Assembly, who shall serve unless they are removed by a two-thirds majority of the Assembly.

The Court shall be responsible for the interpretation of the constitution of the Commonwealth, and for adjudicating on matters referred to it by the Council or the Assembly.

Article 15

THE HUMAN RIGHTS COMMISSION

The Assembly shall elect, at the beginning of each term, from amongst its own Members, a Human Rights Commission, composed of persons from each Member State who shall serve for the duration of that term.

That Commission, guided by the Charter of Rights set out below, shall have the authority to examine and report on any matter which it deems to involve human rights throughout the Commonwealth, or any matter referred to it by the Assembly, the Council or the Secretariat, and all its reports shall be published.

The Council, the Assembly and any Member State whose practices have been examined by the Commission shall consider and publish their response to such recommendations as may be made by the Commission.

Article 16

THE SECRETARIAT

There shall be a Secretary-General of the Commonwealth, elected by the Assembly at the beginning of its term, who shall serve for four years, and who shall have responsibility for the administration of the Commonwealth, reporting jointly to the Council and the Assembly.

The Secretariat shall consist of a number of deputy Secretaries-General who shall be nominated by the Secretary-General and confirmed by the Assembly, and by a full-time staff for whom the Secretary-General shall be responsible.

The Secretary-General, or his deputies, shall attend all meetings of the Council of Ministers and the Assembly, may make recommendations to those bodies, and shall implement decisions taken by the institutions of the Commonwealth.

The costs of administration of the Commonwealth shall be met by moneys provided by the Member States through an equitable tax system levied within each state for that purpose.

Article 17

THE RIGHTS OF MEMBER STATES

Nothing in this Treaty shall infringe the absolute legal rights of Member States to take such action, within their own jurisdiction, which they believe to be necessary, using such powers as they possess.

The government of each Member State shall, subject to the consent of its parliament, implement any Convention or Treaty to which it has become a signatory on its own initiative or on the initiative of the Commonwealth.

Article 18

RIGHTS OF THE PEOPLES OF THE COMMONWEALTH

The rights of the peoples of the Commonwealth to elect or remove their own governments, and as a result, to repeal or amend their own domestic legislation or to follow such policies as may have been determined by their own parliaments and governments, shall be entrenched in this Treaty.

Article 19

DOMESTIC JURISDICTION OF COURTS OF MEMBER STATES

Nothing in this Treaty shall in any way limit the powers of the Courts of Member States to apply the domestic laws of their own states in accordance with their own constitutional arrangements.

Article 20

RATIFICATION AND AMENDMENT OF THE TREATY

This Treaty shall be ratified by a referendum to be held in each Member State, and may be amended, on the recommendation of a majority of the Council of Ministers and the Assembly, subject to the approval of all the Member States by a popular vote in a referendum in each Member State.

ANNEXE—THE CHARTER OF RIGHTS

1. All citizens shall be entitled to enjoy, and to campaign for, universal democratic and enforceable rights, both individual and collective, enshrined in law, adhered to in practice and respected by society, as a precondition of self-government and the achievement of full political, social and economic emancipation within a civilized society.

2. Every citizen shall have the following political rights:

—to freedom of speech;

—to freedom of assembly and of association for the purpose of expressing an opinion, without interference from the State;

—to organize for common political, social or economic ends;

—to practise, or not to practise, any or all religions;

—to vote in all elections, participate in all electoral processes and institutions, and to contest all elections;

—to privacy and the protection of personal information and correspondence from surveillance or interference;

—to information about public, political, social or economic affairs;

—to freedom of movement, unhindered by arbitrary interference, and to be given asylum from political, social or economic oppression; and

—to conscientious objection to service in the armed forces.

3. Every citizen shall have the following legal rights:

—to personal freedom from arbitrary arrest, detention or harassment;

—to a fair and impartial hearing by a jury of the citizen's peers if accused of any unlawful activity, and to equal treatment before the law and equal access to legal representation;

—to be presumed innocent until proved guilty, to be informed of all charges laid and the evidence in support of them, and the right to silence in court;

—to freedom from torture or cruel and degrading treatment, and from capital punishment;

—to legal advice and services, free at the point of use; and

—to equal treatment before the law, and in the community, without discrimination, and regardless of race, sex or sexual preference, colour, religious or political conviction or disability.

4. Every citizen shall have the following social rights:

—to adequate and warm housing and comfortable living conditions;

—to rest, recreation and leisure, to a limitation of working hours and to holidays;

—to enjoy access to literature, music, the arts and cultural activities;

—to good health care and preventive medicine, free at the moment of need;

—to lifelong and free educational provision;

—to dignity and care in retirement;

—in the case of women, to control of their own fertility and reproduction;

—to free and equal access to child care;

—to cheap, effective and equitable means of transportation;

—to a healthy, sustainable, accessible and attractive environment and to clean water and air;

—to media free from governmental or commercial domination; and

—to full access to personal information held by any public authority, subject only to a restriction order signed by a Minister and reported to Parliament.

5. Every citizen shall have the following economic rights:

—to useful work at a fair wage that provides an income sufficient to maintain a decent standard of living;

Appendix 3
Oaths

The Coronation Oath

The Queen having returned to her Chair, (her Majesty having already on Tuesday, the 4th day of November, 1952, in the presence of the two Houses of Parliament, made and signed the Declaration prescribed by Act of Parliament), the Archbishop standing before her shall administer the Coronation Oath, first asking the Queen,

Madam, is your Majesty willing to take the Oath?

And the Queen answering,

I am willing.

The Archbishop shall minister these questions; and the Queen, having a book in her hands, shall answer each question severally as follows:

Archbishop: Will you solemnly promise and swear to govern the Peoples of the United Kingdom of Great Britain and Northern Ireland, Canada, Australia, New Zealand, the Union of South Africa, Pakistan, and Ceylon, and of your Possessions and the other Territories to any of them belonging or pertaining, according to their respective laws and customs?

Queen: I solemnly promise so to do.

Archbishop: Will you to your power cause Law and Justice, in Mercy, to be executed in all your judgements?

Queen: I will.

Archbishop: Will you to the utmost of your power maintain the Laws of God and the true profession of the

Gospel? Will you to the utmost of your power maintain in the United Kingdom the Protestant Reformed Religion established by law? Will you maintain and preserve inviolably the settlement of the Church of England, and the doctrine, worship, discipline, and government thereof, as by law established in England? And will you preserve unto the Bishops and Clergy of England, and to the Churches there committed to their charge, all such rights and privileges, as by law do or shall appertain to them or any of them?

Queen: All this I promise to do.

Then the Queen arising out of her Chair, supported as before, the Sword of State being carried before her, shall go to the Altar, and make her solemn Oath in the sight of all the people to observe the premisses: laying her right hand upon the Holy Gospel in the great Bible (which was before carried in the procession and is now brought from the Altar by the Archbishop, and tendered to her as she kneels upon the steps), and saying these words:

The things which I have here before promised, I will perform and keep. So help me God.

Then the Queen shall kiss the Book and sign the Oath.

The Oath of Allegiance for the Armed Forces

I..Swear by Almighty God that I will be faithful and bear true allegiance to Her Majesty Queen Elizabeth II Her Heirs and Successors and that I will as in duty bound honestly and faithfully defend Her Majesty, Her Heirs and Successors, in Person, Crown and Dignity against all enemies and will observe and obey all orders of Her Majesty, Her Heirs and Successors and of the Generals and Officers set over me.

The Bishops' Oath

Homage

I

HAVING BEEN ELECTED, CONFIRMED AND CONSECRATED
BISHOP OF
DO HEREBY DECLARE
THAT YOUR MAJESTY IS THE ONLY SUPREME GOVERNOR OF
THIS YOUR REALM
IN SPIRITUAL AND ECCLESIASTICAL THINGS
AS WELL AS IN TEMPORAL
AND THAT NO FOREIGN PRELATE OR POTENTATE
HAS ANY JURISDICTION WITHIN THIS REALM
AND I ACKNOWLEDGE THAT I HOLD THE SAID BISHOPRIC
AS WELL THE SPIRITUALITIES AS THE TEMPORALITIES
THEREOF
ONLY OF YOUR MAJESTY
AND FOR THE SAME TEMPORALITIES I DO MY HOMAGE PRES-
ENTLY TO YOUR MAJESTY
SO HELP ME GOD
GOD SAVE QUEEN ELIZABETH

NB. A SLIGHT PAUSE SHOULD BE MADE AT THE END OF EACH
LINE.

The Privy Councillors' Oath★

You do swear by Almighty God that you will be faithful and bear true Allegiance to His Majesty King George the Sixth, His Heirs and Successors according to Law.
SO HELP YOU GOD.

You do swear by Almighty God to be a true and faithful Servant unto the King's Majesty, as one of His Majesty's Privy Council. You will not know or understand of any manner of thing to be attempted, done, or spoken against His Majesty's Person, Honour, Crown, or Dignity Royal, but you will lett and withstand the same to the uttermost of your Power, and either cause it to be revealed to His Majesty Himself, or to such of His Privy Council as shall advertise His Majesty of the same. You will, in all things to be moved, treated, and debated in Council, faithfully and truly declared your Mind and Opinion, according to your Heart and Conscience; and will keep secret all Matters committed and revealed unto you, or that shall be treated of secretly in Council. And if any of the said Treaties or Counsels shall touch any of the Counsellors, you will not reveal it unto him, but will keep the same until such time as, by the Consent of His Majesty, or of the Council, Publication shall be made thereof. You will to your uttermost bear Faith and Allegiance unto the King's Majesty; and will assist and defend all Jurisdictions, Pre-eminences, and Authorities, granted to His Majesty, and annexed to the Crown by Acts of Parliament, or otherwise against all Foreign Princes, Persons, Prelates, States, or Potentates. And Generally in all things you will do as a faithful and true Servant ought to do to His Majesty.
SO HELP YOU GOD.

★ This oath remains unchanged under Queen Elizabeth II except that Privy Councillors may now affirm and not swear.

The EC Commissioners' Oath

Solemn declaration made by commissioners before the Court of Justice

I solemnly undertake:

To perform my duties in complete independence, in the general interest of the Communities;

In carrying out my duties, neither to seek nor to take instructions from any Government or body;

To refrain from any action incompatible with my duties.

I formally note the undertaking of each Member State to respect this principle and not to seek to influence Members of the Commission in the performance of their task.

I further undertake to respect, both during and after my term of office, the obligations arising therefrom, and in particular the duty to behave with integrity and discretion as regards the acceptance, after I have ceased to hold office, of certain appointments or benefits.

Parliamentary Oaths
(taken from Sir Thomas Erskine May's Parliamentary Practice)

The occupants of the government front bench (see p.235) are the first to be sworn, and after them the occupants of the opposition front bench. Where these and any privy counsellors not included among them have taken the oath the Speaker calls the other Members present bench by bench, giving precedence to the various benches at his discretion, but as a rule calling those on his right and those on his left alternately (H. C. Deb. (1935–36) 307, c. 13).

On the following day the daily prayers are read, for the first time, by Mr. Speaker's chaplain; and the Speaker, if the necessity arises, counts the House, and cannot take the chair unless forty members are present, as the oath must, under Section 3 of the Parliamentary Oaths Act, 1866, be taken whilst a full House of Commons is duly sitting with their Speaker in his chair.

The Members continue to take the oath on that day, after which the greater part are sworn and qualified to sit and vote.

Oath on demise of Crown.—In the event of the demise of the Crown Parliament meets immediately, pursuant to the Succession to the Crown Act, 1707, and all Members of both Houses again take the oath (*m*).

There appears to be some doubt whether the obligation to take the oath in these circumstances is statutory or rests merely upon the custom of Parliament. The latter opinion has been stated with authority in the House of Commons (H. C. Deb. (1937) 319, c. 762).

On the death of Edward VII the House of Commons met on Saturday, May 1910, but, owing to the unavoidable absence of the Speaker, the Chairman of Ways and Means and the Deputy Chairman, adjourned to the following Monday when the Chairman of Ways and Means acting as Deputy Speaker and other Members took the oath (C. J. (1910) 147). The Speaker took the oath at the first sitting of the House at which he was present (C. J. (1919) 154).

Manner of taking the oath.—The Promissory Oaths Act, 1868, substituted for various earlier forms the oath

---

(*m*) L.J. (1937) 420, etc.; C.J. (1837) 490, etc.; L.J. (1901) 4, etc.; C.J. (1901) 5, etc.; L.J. (1910) 121, etc.; C.J. (1910) 150, etc.; L.J. (1935–36) 51, etc.; C.J. (1935–36) 50, etc.; L.J. (1936–37) 59, etc.; C.J. (1936–37) 59; L.J. (1951–52) 77; C.J. (1951–52) 88.

which with the necessary alteration in the sovereign's designation (*n*) is now in the following form: "I —— do swear that I will be faithful and bear true allegiance to Her Majesty Queen Elizabeth, her heirs and successors, according to law, So help me God" (*o*).

A Member who desires to do so may take the oath in this form and kiss the book, but the ordinary form and manner of administering and taking the oath are prescribed by section 2 of the Oaths Act, 1909. Under this section the person taking the oath holds the New Testament, or, in the case of a Jew, the Old Testament, in his uplifted hand, and says or repeats after the officer administering the oath the words, "I swear by Almighty God that . . ." followed by the words of the oath prescribed by law. A Member may also take the oath with uplifted hand in the manner usually followed in Scotland (*p*).

Affirmation in lieu of oath.—Members who object to be sworn may avail themselves of the power granted by section 1 of the Oaths Act, 1888 (*q*), which enacts that a solemn affirmation may be made in lieu of an oath by every person who states, as the ground of such objection, either that he has not religious belief or that the taking of such an oath is contrary to his religious belief.

Time for taking the oath.—A definite time at the beginning of a sitting is reserved for Members returned after a general election who desire to take the oath or make

---

(*n*) Promissory Oaths, 1868, s. 10.
(*o*) Promissory Oaths Act, 1868, ss. 2, 8.
(*p*) Oaths Act, 1888, s. 5.
(*q*) See also S. O. No. 99.

the affirmation required by law on any day after the days set aside for taking the oath (r) (see p. 365).

Penalties for omission to take the oath.—By the Acts 30 Chas. 2, stat. 2; 13 Will. 3, c. 6; and 1 Geo. 1, stat. 2, c. 13, severe penalties and disabilities were inflicted upon any Member of either House who sat or voted without having taken the oath. By the Parliamentary Oaths Act, 1866, any Peer voting by himself or his proxy, or sitting in the House of Peers without having taken the oath, is subject for every such offence, to a penalty of 500*l*.; and any Member of the House of Commons who votes as such, or sits during any debate after the Speaker has been chosen, without having taken the oath, is subject to the same penalty, and his seat is also vacated in the same manner as if he were dead. These penalties can be recovered upon the suit of the Crown alone (s). When Peers or Members have neglected to take the oaths from haste, accident, or inadvertence, Acts of indemnity have been passed to relieve them from the consequences of their neglect (t). In the Commons, however, it is necessary to move a new writ immediately the omission is discovered, as the Member's seat is vacated (u).

(r) C. J. (1886) 5; Parl. Deb. (1886) 302, c. 21. On 9 March 1882, the Speaker had stated that to object to any Member taking the oath except on grounds public or notorious, or within the cognizance of the House, would be simply vexatious, Parl. Deb. (1882) 267, c. 442.

(s) *Bradlaugh* v. *Clarke* (1883), 8 App. Cas. 354.

(t) 45 Geo. 3, c. 5 (Lord J. Thynne); 56 Geo. 3, c. 48 (Earl Gower); I Will, 4, c. 8 (Lord R. Grosvenor); 5 Vict. c. 3 (Earl of Scarborough); Lord Plunket and Lord Byron 1880, private Acts (not printed). In recent cases in the House of Lords, Acts of Indemnity have not been introduced. Four peers having sat and voted in session 1906 without having taken the oath (Parl. Deb. (1906) 163, c. 1291; *ibid*. 164, c. 4), the matter was referred to the select committee on the Standing Orders of the House in 1907 (see L. J. (1907) 105; H. L. 95, p. iv (1907)).

(u) C. J. (1805–06) 148; *ibid*. (1812) 286; *ibid*. (1813–14) 144; *ibid*. (1816–17) 42; *ibid*. (1830) 353; *ibid*. (1924) 74. In Mr. Bradlaugh's case the Chiltern Hundreds (see p. 212) were accepted.